Creating Welcoming Schools

A Practical Guide to Home–School Partnerships with Diverse Families

Creating Welcoming Schools

A Practical Guide to Home–School Partnerships with Diverse Families

JoBeth Allen

FOREWORD BY CONCHA DELGADO-GAITAN

Teachers College, Columbia University
New York and London

INTERNATIONAL
Reading Association
800 BARKSDALE ROAD, PO BOX 8139
NEWARK, DE 19714-8139, USA (302) 731-1600
www.reading.org

Published simultaneously by Teachers College Press, 1234 Amsterdam Avenue, New York, NY 10027 and The International Reading Association, 800 Barksdale Road, Newark, DE 19714.

All photos by Jan Miller Burkins except Chapter 4, which is by Monira Al-Haroun.

Library of Congress Cataloging-in-Publication Data

Allen, JoBeth.
    Creating welcoming schools : a practical guide to home–school partnerships with diverse families / JoBeth Allen ; foreword by Concha Delgado-Gaitan.
      p. cm.
    Includes bibliographical references and index.
    ISBN-13: 978-0-8077-4790-2 (hardcover)
    ISBN-10: 0-8077-4790-4 (hardcover)
    ISBN-13: 978-0-8077-4789-6 (pbk.)
    ISBN-10: 0-8077-4789-0 (pbk.)
    1. Home and school—United States.   2. Parent-teacher relationships—United States.   3. Education—Parent participation—United States.   4. United States—Ethnic relations.   I. Title.
    LC225.3.A45 2006
    371.19'2—dc22
                                                                        2007000232
ISBN: 978-0-8077-4789-6 (paper)
ISBN: 978-0-8077-4790-2 (cloth)

IRA inventory number 9219

Printed on acid-free paper

Manufactured in the United States of America

14 13 12 11 10   8 7 6 5 4 3

Contents

Foreword

Long before I researched issues of school–community relationships, I was convinced that learning was a family and school partnership. Both of my parents spoke limited English and neither had formal schooling in Mexico. That didn't stop my mother from showing up with armloads of cupcakes for our classroom on Fridays when she was the "room mother." She was a strong and visible influence in my school and home life. It mattered to me that my mother held high expectations for my sisters and me to succeed in school; I knew that I had to try my best. Nothing short of an excellent report from the teacher was acceptable for Mom.

Later, as an elementary teacher and then a school principal, I enlisted parental support for our educational programs. The challenges were many because in our communities, families were culturally diverse and lived in poverty conditions.

As an ethnographic researcher, I document how children from culturally diverse families who live in impoverished conditions can succeed in school when their family and school collaborate on their behalf. I've appreciated how cultural and socioeconomic differences bear on children's educational opportunities. Parents from poor communities value education for their children, in spite of the lack of financial, social, and political resources. However, poor nutrition and inferior health care as well as inadequate housing can negatively affect children's school attendance. These social conditions often defeat children's motivation and opportunity to learn.

Although adverse environments can prevent parents from participating in schools, this is not due to cultural dictates. A misperception in the mainstream system is that culturally diverse families are culturally deficient, preventing them from participating in their children's schooling. In actuality, the major reasons that parents do not participate in schools are primarily structural: Schools either include or exclude parents. In this book, JoBeth Allen shows us how inclusion is possible through effective partnerships between schools and communities.

Besides her scholarly contribution, Allen's uniqueness is in the integrity with which she walks us into everyday settings where diversity thrives.

She leads us into critical niches where effective school–community partnerships reside. In communities from coast to coast, we meet school and
community leaders who are exemplary partners. They reach beyond differences and obstacles to connect with each other for the students' benefit.
In her book *Peripheral Visions* (1994), anthropologist Mary Catherine Bateson
writes: "The basic challenge we face today in an interdependent world is
to disconnect the notion of difference from the notion of superiority, to turn
the unfamiliar into a resource rather than a threat"(p. 233). Successful partnerships can accomplish this adjustment.

Allen's stories open doors for us to enter and learn how communities
struggle to respond to diversity and in the process learn new skills to
organize family–school partnerships. One example where we see those
connections is in the Verde Involving Parents (VIP) Program at Verde Elementary School. Family partners made home visits and supported families to resolve underlying problems preventing students from succeeding
in school. Educators reading about Verde and other settings will carry away
an important lesson: Partnerships succeed when schools utilize local services and resources to make sustained structural changes for their children,
school, and the community.

If you are an educational researcher, teacher educator, or educator
directly and indirectly involved with students in public schools, this book
belongs on your required reading list. After all, democracy works only
when families fully commit to their children's education alongside the
schools, and when the schools fully involve culturally diverse families.
Students depend on the total support of their family and their community,
compelling us to partner and build strong educational settings. We cannot
afford not to.

—*Concha Delgado-Gaitan*

REFERENCE

Bateson, M. C. (1994). *Peripheral visons: Learning along the way.* New York: Harper
    Collins.

Acknowledgments

Never does an event, a fact, a deed, a gesture of rage or love, a poem, a painting, a song, a book, have only one reason behind it
—Freire, 1994, p. 10

The book has a host of reasons behind it, mentors both near and distant. I have learned so much about relationships with families from my close collaboration with teacher researchers Betty Shockley Bisplinghoff and Barbara Michalove. Our collaborative action research, first in *Engaging Children* (1993) and then in *Engaging Families* (1995), taught me much of what I've shared in these pages. It also led to the wonderful study group PhOLKS (Photographs of Local Knowledge Sources); these educators—Vinette Fabregas, Karen Hankins, Greg Hull, Linda Labbo, Hattie Lawson, Barbara Michalove, Steve Piazza, Cyndi Piha, Linda Sprague, Sybil Townsend, and Carmen Urdanivia-English—taught me about family funds of knowledge in my own community. The book is informed by the astute insights of my colleagues Jan Miller Burkins and Betsy Rymes; we traded chapters as they wrote outstanding books on literacy coaching and classroom discourse analysis, respectively.

Other near mentors are educators I've had the privilege of advising during their doctoral studies. One of the reasons I decided to write this book is to share the excellent work they have done, and continue to do, in forming relationships with families in ways that deeply support student learning. Thank you to my students/my teachers, including Karen Hankins, Shane Rayburn, Carmen Uranivia-English, Teri Holbrook, and Jane Rogers, whose work you will read in these pages. Thank you as well to current students/teachers who provided feedback at various stages of this process.

Nearest of all and providing perhaps the most pressing reason for my abiding passion for home–school connections are my grown children, Rachel, Luke, and Paul. They read "their" parts and agreed to share them —even the hard parts—with readers.

More distant mentors are Sarah Lawrence-Lightfoot, whose insightful and compassionate conversations with teachers and parents were indeed essential; and Norma Gonzáles, Luis Moll, and Cathy Amanti, who awakened educators throughout the country to the valuable resources of family funds of knowledge and respectful partnerships for student learning. Others who have forged those relationships—such as Alma Flor Ada, Isabel Campoy, Linda Winston, Concha Delgado-Gaitan, Deborah Dixon, and Jeanne Paratore—have inspired me.

All these mentors, and others whose work I draw on throughout the book, have urged me to pursue Freire's eloquent challenge. Humanity lies, he wrote, in the "restless, impatient, continuing, hopeful inquiry" we pursue "in the world, with the world, and with each other" (1970, p. 58).

Welcoming All Families

On a golden October morning in a quiet residential neighborhood, as I signed in at the front office of a local elementary school to visit a colleague, a mom, a dad, and a young boy stood somewhat tentatively behind me. "Yes?" asked the secretary, glancing at them briefly. The father introduced himself and said softly that the child was transferring to the school. "I know," said the secretary, just a hint of irritation in her otherwise flat tone. "We were expecting him yesterday. And school starts at 7:45." It was 9:30.

Hers was the first face of the school, the first voice connecting that family and that school. There was no "We are so glad to have you in our school. I'll bet it was hard to leave your friends at Eastside School," or, "Hello, Pablo! Your new classmates are eager to meet you. Let me take you down to your room." Was the secretary tired that morning? Was this student, transferring from a "failing" school in the system, unwelcome? Would the greeting have been different if the parents had identified themselves as professors, if the parents' English had not been accented (or had, perhaps, a French accent), or if Pablo's standardized test scores had preceded him and were in the highest quartile?

This school, like many schools all over the country, worked for months to write a school improvement plan. A major component of that plan was a column labeled "Parental Involvement." Goals included statements like "Increase parent participation in PTO by 5% per year for the next 3 years," and "By Year 3, every teacher will have 100% participation in parent–teacher conferences." Strategies included having parents sign contracts to ensure their support of their child's learning, hiring parent liaisons, translating notes home into Spanish, getting businesses to donate food for evening events ("They always come when we have hot dogs or spaghetti"), and offering parenting classes such as *Discipline with Love* and *Reading to Your Child*.

This is a good school in many ways—perhaps it is even like your school. There is a dedicated faculty: there is a record of solid achievement—this school is never at the bottom of the column when test scores are listed in the paper (and on real estate agents' "information about schools" sheets). But in the past few years teachers have seen the neighborhood (and the test scores) change. The school is becoming more ethnically, economically, and linguistically diverse. Teachers state their commitment to providing the best possible education for every child, and they know that "getting parents involved" is correlated with school success.

But teachers in this school and many schools throughout the country are struggling with how to be truly welcoming to the diverse families they serve. More than 90% of the teachers in the United States are European American; about 70% are women; and most are comfortably middle class (not wealthy, mind you). Student populations, however, are increasingly diverse. Through tremendous effort and ongoing reflection some teachers and schools have found ways of inviting parents into genuine partnerships. This book is an invitation to read about these efforts, to discuss them in your school, and to work in collaboration with families to create respectful partnerships in your school—relationships that support and enhance the learning of every child.

IF YOU ARE READING THIS BOOK

As a reader of this book, you may be one or more of the following:

- A teacher who cares deeply about your students. You want your school to be welcoming to all families.

- A parent who is committed to your child and to his or her school. You want your family to be a partner with your school in educating your child.
- A member of a group of teachers and parents committed to reading, talking, and acting together to form strong partnerships as co-educators of your children. Maybe you are reading this in your site-based school council, as a committee working on a meaningful family engagement plan as part of No Child Left Behind, or as a PTA.
- A college student studying to become the best teacher you can be. Your professors keep talking about respecting diversity and about how important parent involvement is—but what does it look like?
- An administrator in a diverse school or district who knows that there is no one program, no quick fix, for building lasting partnerships among families, schools, and the community.

This book encourages building partnerships between home and school that support each child's learning and development, whether he is 3 and leaving the nest for the first time, or she is 18 and leaving it for good. As I learned about genuine home and school partnerships with my colleagues Betty Shockley and Barbara Michalove, partnerships are different from "parent involvement programs":

> Programs are implemented; partnerships are developed. Programs are adopted; partnerships are constructed. . . . By their very nature, most programs have steps, elements, or procedures that become static. A program cannot constantly reinvent itself, change with each year, be different in every classroom, and for every teacher-family-child relationship. (Shockley, Michalove, & Allen, 1995, p. 91)

EXAMINING FAMILY–SCHOOL RELATIONSHIPS

Why do we need to reexamine the relationships between families and schools? Isn't there a natural alliance of adults who have at heart the welfare of the children they share? Let's take a look at some examples from cyberspace. This first one is from a blog that is no longer active by Teri Holbrook, the mother of two, with one child diagnosed with dyslexia and another with giftedness:

> It's Sunday at 5:50, and we all are a bit down. My younger daughter keeps coming over to me for a hug. "I don't like Sunday afternoons," she says. "They mean Monday is coming soon." I give her a

squeeze. I know what she means. Come Monday, and we put on our game faces. We have to do school again.

We crave these times away from school, even the child who is undiluted in her label as gifted. At home, we look at each other with the relief of recognition. We don't have to be the good student or the bad student, the good parent or the bad parent. We don't have to be the family who gets the phone calls and the notes home; the family who spends either too little or too much time on homework; the rebellious, quirky family who doesn't seem to fit. We get to just be us, tumbled together in our house, content with our para-schooled selves. Soon it will be dinnertime, and we'll tell jokes around the table and discuss what game we'll play after the dishes are cleaned. We'll cling to Sunday evening as long as we can.

What a negative mom, we teachers may be tempted to think. I'll bet her daughters don't have a very positive attitude about school. She doesn't say "teachers" but she obviously thinks we are ruining her family life. It's parents like her who make our jobs so difficult. Doesn't she know we are doing everything we can for both her daughters and that we really want to work with her on their behalf? Teri, my colleague, sent me the following website (http://www.tard-blog.com/) from a special-education "teacher" who has since quit teaching, perhaps run out by the real teachers in her school:

> I am a special education teacher. Unfortunately, a lot of the parents don't care about their kids, especially the parents of my special education students. I say this because only about seven out of twenty parents actually come to their scheduled parent/teacher conference.
>
> It is often a relief that some parents do not come. Coming up with nice things to say about their kids is always tough. Basically, I have to lie to their faces and end up feeding them a load of BS. I do this for two reasons. First, I have so many negative things to say about them and their children, that throwing in a positive every now and then alleviates the tension during these conferences. Second, I force myself to say nice things so the parents don't go home and beat their kid's ass. . . .
>
> Only one of the parents showed up today to meet with me out of the six I had scheduled. And I am convinced that the only reason this mother showed up was because we have called Child Protective Services on her so many times, that she now fears losing her daughter, who is the mother's meal ticket to government aid.
>
> A few things you should know about this mother . . .
>
> • She works at a convenience store.
> • She has two kids from two different fathers, and has never been married.

- She lives with her two kids in a low income-housing complex.
- Her daughter, who is in my class, was born addicted to crack-cocaine and with fetal alcohol syndrome. (http://www.tard-blog.com/)

Few teachers are this blatantly hostile, but it takes only one or two encounters with educators who do not respect them or their children for parents to feel alienated from schools. A school counselor in Houston blamed low student achievement on parents, whom he called "a bunch of seventh-grade dropouts who can't add 2 plus 2" (*Houston Chronicle*, 1998, p. 21A, cited in Patterson, Baldwin, Gonzales, Guadarrama, & Keith, 1999). The February 21, 2005, cover story of *Time* magazine was, "What Teachers Hate About Parents." A call for research from the editor of an educational journal asked, "Can we change parenting behaviors? If so, which ones should we change?"

I don't know about you, but as a parent and an educator I am insulted. Who are "we," and what right do "we" have to tell parents to change their behaviors?

Annette Lareau (2003) and her colleagues spent hundreds of hours observing and interviewing poor, working-class, and middle-class parents to learn about the lives of their children, aged 9 and 10. They also interviewed the children's teachers. Listen to what two teachers in very different schools said about parents:

> An unsupportive parent is one who is antagonistic with the teacher. . . . And it makes the job virtually impossible. If you have a problem with the child, the parent is not supportive of you or the school's position. And the child is at odds with you, and they fight you tooth and nail, and they basically say, "I don't have to listen to you; [I] don't have to do what you say."

> [Parents have] gotten this attitude now where they question so much. The children see and hear this. Then they come to your classroom with an attitude. Not many, but you can sure pick it up right away. Some of them are very surly. . . . I think a lot of if comes from home. (p. 27)

One of the interesting things about these two quotes is that they are from teachers serving very different populations—one middle- to upper-class, the other working-class and poor students. Can you tell which is which? Throughout the book, Lareau (2003) noted that while some teachers were highly supportive of parents, others had somewhat contradictory expectations. They want parents to be deferential and supportive of school policies and decisions, but they also want parents to "take leadership roles in solving their children's educational problems" (p. 27). As you can imagine, these expectations sometimes leave parents confused, frustrated, or downright angry. For their part, parents expressed many expectations of the teachers and schools:

> Some of the teachers are just not doing a good job. They can't explain things. I think some of them are setting the kids up for failure. (p. 193)

> I had a negative opinion [about Mr. I] from the parents. They don't like his teaching methods. They don't like his gruffness. People didn't like Ms. [H.] . . . because she was very old-school and had not changed or adapted her teaching. Her classroom was very boring. (p. 187)

> I hate the school. I hate it. I tried to get him into Catholic . . . but they said they didn't have any room for him so it's like every day of my life I'm struggling to get this kid straightened out. It's my life. (p. 227)

Cheryl Fields-Smith (2005), an African American woman who has been both a teacher and a parent, learned from interviewing 19 African American parents, whose children attended five different schools in the urban southeast, that they were very involved with their children's education. They believed it was their responsibility to initiate relationships with the school; they volunteered and supported teachers in a variety of ways. The reason many gave, however, was based on a distrust of schools to act in the best interests of their children. The majority indicated "a need to watch over teacher–child interactions" and "frequent accounts of having to advocate on behalf of their children—and other people's children—at the classroom level" (p. 133).

FAMILY–SCHOOL PARTNERSHIPS THAT MAKE A DIFFERENCE

I suspect you are reading this book for the same reason I wrote it—because we all believe that parental involvement leads to student achievement. But that ain't necessarily so, according to Mattingly, Radmila, McKenzie, Rodriguez, and Kayzar (2002), who analyzed the evaluations of 41 parental involvement programs. They concluded that what the programs counted as parental involvement didn't *necessarily* improve student achievement.

But there is more to the story, and it is quite good news. What the research is telling us is that we need to focus our efforts differently, that our well-intentioned plans to increase parental involvement in traditional "get them to the school" events are missing the critical connection among educators, families, and students. Let's look at parental involvement through a more focused lens: What happens when parents are actively engaged with their children outside school in activities designed to enhance academic performance? That is how Nye, Turner, and Schwartz (n.d.) defined pa-

rental involvement in their review of 18 studies in a variety of school settings. They found a statistically significant positive effect from this kind of
direct parental involvement on student academic performance, especially
in reading development.

In another important analysis of research, Anne Henderson and
Karen Mapp (2002) examined 80 studies of parental involvement, preschool through high school, in settings throughout the United States. They
concluded that "the evidence is consistent, positive, and convincing: many
forms of family and community involvement influence student achievement at all ages" (p. 7) and across cultural groups.

The critical factor was that parental involvement had to be related to
their children's academic learning, as evident in Henderson and Mapp's
(2002) key findings:

- Programs and interventions that *engage families in supporting their
  children's learning at home* are linked to improved student achievement.
- *The more families support their children's learning and educational progress,*
  both in quantity and over time, *the more their children tend to do well in
  school and continue their education.*
- *Families of all cultural backgrounds, education, and income levels can, and
  often do, have a positive influence on their children's learning.*
- Family and community involvement that is *linked to student learning has a greater effect on achievement* than more general forms of
  involvement.

A second critical conclusion Henderson and Mapp (2002) reached was
that "when programs and initiatives focus on *building respectful and trusting relationships* among school staff, families, and community members, they
are more effective in creating and sustaining connections that *support
student achievement*" (p. 43, emphasis added). Across studies the authors
learned that:

- Programs that successfully connect with families and community
  *invite involvement, are welcoming, and address specific parental and com-
  munity needs.*
- Parent involvement programs that are effective in engaging diverse
  families *recognize cultural and class differences, address needs, and build
  on strengths.*
- Effective connections *embrace a philosophy of partnership where power
  is shared*—the responsibility for children's educational development
  is a collaborative enterprise among parents, school staff, and community members.

- Organized initiatives to *build parent and community leadership aimed at improving low-performing schools* are growing and leading to promising results in low-income urban areas and the rural South.

Just as teachers have come to reject "reading readiness" as authentic literacy instruction, so we need to reject many indicators of parental involvement that are not authentic. Circling a spider whose mouth is turned upside down in a row of smiling arachnids on a "readiness" worksheet is not reading. Likewise, counting the number of parents who come to PTA meetings, bring cookies to parties, or sign reading logs is not the kind of parental involvement that leads to increased academic development.

If we don't accept the "common knowledge" that parental involvement of any kind increases student learning, we need to look deeper at what kind of relationships between home and school and among parents, teachers, and students might really make a difference. Psychologist and co-founder of Head Start Urie Bronfenbrenner (1994) developed a model of human learning and development that emphasizes that humans don't develop in isolation, but in relation to their environments of family and home, school, community, and society. Each of these changing and multilevel environments interacts with the others, and that interaction can support or impede development. Before Bronfenbrenner, child psychologists studied children, educators studied learning, sociologists focused on families, anthropologists researched culture, political scientists explicated policy—you get the picture or, rather, pieces of the picture. No one studied the whole.

Bronfenbrenner's genius was to look at each part of the social systems (homes, schools, parental workplaces, community economies, and so forth) as they interacted. He theorized that it was the unique interaction of these systems that had an impact on each child. He argued that growth is facilitated when there are strong, positive, and consistent links between settings (e.g., home and school). Children need links—links created by their families and their teachers—that are positive, that develop mutual trust, that create shared goals, and that share power and responsibility on behalf of the child. The key to building this trusting, positive relationship between people in different settings (i.e., family members and educators) is two-way communication. Specifically, Bronfenbrenner (1994) argued that children show the most growth in the transition between primary settings when "valid information, advice, and experience relevant to one setting are made available, on a continuing basis, to the other" (p. 217). Families share information and advice with teachers. Teachers share with parents. Children benefit.

We've seen this in our own children and in others when they have transitioned from home to kindergarten, from elementary to middle and then high school, from school in one town to another—even if it's just from school to the city recreation program. As parents and teachers, we have been so grateful when there is a good support system and good communication, when educators and families and community agencies all seem to be working together on behalf of the child. And we have seen the devastating effects when this web of caring and communicating disintegrates.

As educators, we work hard to provide parents information, advice, and commentary on our students through newsletters, parent–teacher conferences, report cards, and school-based programs. It has been harder to learn from parents their information, advice, and experiences with their children that will help us be more effective teachers. This book is an attempt to spin strands of communication from which we can weave a web of caring that supports each child, each teacher, and each family, so that all children learn to their full potentials.

READING THIS BOOK TOGETHER

In Chapter 1 we'll do some storytelling to explore our own memories of schooling. We'll dig a little deeper in Chapter 2 to examine our cultural influences—what came together in those certain times and places of our childhood and adulthood to make us who we are, and how can understanding our own cultural lives help us understand others? Understanding and learning about the lives of other families—especially the families of the children in the school in which you teach—is the focus of Chapter 3. Then in Chapter 4 we'll explore various pathways to learning family funds of knowledge through photography, cultural informants, and individual teacher–student–family relationships.

Creating dialogue—one of the most difficult and most essential elements of any relationship—is the focus of Chapters 5 through 9. First, in Chapter 5, we examine what genuine dialogue is and how it differs from other kinds of communication, how we establish it, and what happens when it fails. In Chapter 6 we focus on dialogue at parent–teacher conferences (and suggest a third party at the table), and in Chapter 7 we explore opportunities throughout the year for dialogue. Chapter 8 illuminates how two teachers created ongoing dialogue with parents and other family members through dialogue journals, family storytelling, and other two-way communication pathways. Chapter 9 provides additional opportunities for engaging families in literacy and family history projects.

After exploring how to develop strong partnerships among educators, students, and family members, we examine what might happen within those partnerships. Chapter 10 introduces us to partnerships that work toward education for a democratic society through action research, oral history, community action, and service learning projects. Parent groups allow educators and families to advocate and teach together for students and schools, as we'll see in Chapter 11. Finally, in Chapter 12, we push ourselves to the level of partnerships that transform schools for student learning.

Each chapter includes "Action Opportunities." I encourage you to play with these, to redesign them for your own needs, but most of all to entertain these actions together: parents and teachers, grandparents and school psychologists, foster parents and principals, aunts and uncles and secretaries. We'll end this chapter with one that takes us back to Pablo and his parents, and the secretary of a school that really did want to welcome diverse families.

Action Opportunity: Delgado-Gaitan (2004) stressed that "the first step in involving Latino parents is to value Latino parents' language by employing office personnel who can communicate with them by phone and who can translate correspondence that goes to the families" (p. 24). This is equally true of other ethnic and linguistic groups—we all need to see a friendly, understanding, and helpful person when we come to school. Together with your front-office staff, parents, students, and school faculty, ask yourself some questions: How do we greet children? How do we greet adults? Do all people feel equally welcome? How do we communicate when there are language differences? How can we make changes so our school becomes a more welcoming place for diverse families? How can families help us do so?

CHAPTER 1

Exploring Memories of School

I used to tell my kids about this teacher I had when I was in about eighth grade. She was the type of person that if you didn't learn nothing, she not going to let you pass. Before any kid leave out of her class that kid learned how to read. And that showed the kids right then that she really cared, cause some teachers they don't care. And this lady I'm talking about her name was Ms. Downs and she was a great teacher . . . cause she stayed on you. If she figured that you were playing around and stuff she'll let you get away with it for a while, then she'll tell you straight up, hey, you gonna learn before you leave out of my classroom . . . but every kid that went through her [class], they did learn.

(Compton–Lilly, 2003, p. 69)

This memory of school, told by a mother to her son's first-grade teacher, Cathy Compton-Lilly, is a very positive one. Other parents in Cathy's classroom were not so positive in their memories of school. But they all had stories. We all do.

What stories have shaped us—stories of our lives as students, stories that we need to tell or are afraid to tell or have told so often that our children roll their eyes when we start to tell them again? How have we been affected as parents or grandparents or aunties or teachers? Let's take the plunge and explore them together.

A SCHOOL STORY

When I was in second grade, I ran away from school. I got in trouble (there was this little free-for-all when the teacher left the room), was punished by having to sit with the other offenders in a dark auditorium, and just couldn't take the humiliation. I ran to my house and hid under the bed. Uncharacteristically, my mother wasn't at home. My panicked teacher called to tell my mother I was missing, but I answered. After a tearful reconciliation (she was a first-year teacher and probably more scared than I was), I finished the day. My mother, later apprised of the situation, met me after school, and she and the teacher gently admonished me about the dangers and disrespect inherent in my act. They did not scold, berate, or punish me further. It was obvious to us all that I had learned my lesson, that I had "good parents" who would make sure this did not happen again, and that I was a well-behaved child who was unlikely to cause such trouble again.

I wonder what the school's response would have been to Betty Sue if she had run away? Her mom worked at Johnnie's Tavern and her dad didn't seem to be around much. What about Carlos, whose parents harvested crops with his parents from April until June—Carlos, who lived in Mexico the rest of the year? If they had made the same call, had the same conference, would the tone have been the same? Would the adults' eyes have met in quite the same way, subtly signaling a shared understanding and value system?

I grew up in a series of small towns in Oklahoma, Texas, and Kansas. Here are some of the things I "knew" about home and school:

Moms read to their kids, played word and counting games, sang nursery rhymes, and watched with you "Ding Dong School," "Captain Kangaroo," and other TV shows with kids who looked like your White, middle-class family. Somehow along the way you learned to read.

You were supposed to get As. A B was okay if it was in art or music or PE; a C was never okay.

Teachers liked you and they liked your mom, who helped out with school parties, picked you up when you were running a fever, and was home when they called.

When you came home from school, Mom asked about homework. She never forgot. You always did it. Dad looked up from the paper only if you got sassy.

You never got to stay up late on a school night.

Most kids moved to the next grade each year, but there were some families whose kids got held back regularly. You didn't invite them to spend-the-night parties.

There was a "white" school and a "colored" school in my Texas town, although I found out about the latter only by accident.

Mexican kids moved in and out of the schools, and some of the teachers let the "regular" students know through words and facial expressions that they thought the children, often migrant workers, were dirty and not very smart.

I didn't examine these assumptions as a child, but they shaped my expectations as a learner and later as a teacher, as a parent of three children, and as a teacher educator. I'm ashamed to tell you how old I was before I really understood that I had been a product of a segregated school system and before I realized the prejudice behind my teachers' comments about Mexican children, although I do remember feeling very uncomfortable when these teachers made public comments. All children suffer when any child is demeaned. Now as a mother and grandmother, I'm finding it very helpful to examine my assumptions by telling and writing stories about my schooling.

Each of us has tacit assumptions about what a "normal" home environment is like; humans have the tendency to assume that their own experiences are the norm. Your school experiences may have been very different. Perhaps your family struggled financially and you always felt "out of place" at school; you were ignored or punished in school, so you vowed to become a "different" kind of teacher; or you or your parents participated in integrating the schools. Chances are that most of us have some assumptions about what we think "good home lives" look like. Those of us in education can't help but be influenced by our own family's stance toward school. Most of us parents and especially us grandparents went to school when things were very different from schools today: different families, different expectations, different attitudes about the role of parents.

In this chapter we examine those stories of schooling together to lay our assumptions on the table, to connect the families we lived with to the families of the children we are rearing and/or teaching today.

EXPLORING SCHOOL STORIES TOGETHER

We all have stories of school—a teacher we loved or hated, a time when we felt brilliant or stupid, a group of kids who included or taunted us. What can we learn from sharing our stories as teachers and parents?

Karen Hankins was a first-grade teacher in Athens, Georgia, who decided that she had to explore her own family history to understand the families of the children she taught. She wrote with unusual candor about forgotten, hidden, or never-before-discussed events in her own family (Hankins, 1998). Karen made a conscious effort to see the lives of her students with deeper, more personal understandings by looking for parallel experiences among her family and her students' families. Her grandfather's loss of his hand in a mill accident and subsequent alcoholism helped her understand how circumstances of hopelessness can lead people to addiction, as it had in the families of three children in her room with fetal alcohol/cocaine syndrome. Her family's frustrations and denial ("just don't talk about it") about her sister's learning difficulties and devastating school experiences allowed Karen to empathize with children with similar difficulties and their families.

In a section she called "Facing My Prejudices Through My Memoirs," Karen examined early memories of racial separation and discrimination. She noted that she has to go through a process much like what Maya Angelou described: "I envision racism to be like a blanket which sneaks up and covers me at night as I lie sleeping, and each morning when I awake and find it there yet again I must consciously make the effort to pull it off of me" (quoted in McKee, 1988, p. 14). She began to question the ways in which her "missionary mentality" affected her interactions with children and their families.

Karen continued this hard work during a tumultuous year of teaching, as she recounted in *Teaching Through the Storm* (Hankins, 2003). It was 6:00 in the evening the first week of school, and the mother of one of her first-grade students came to her classroom. Karen asked what she wanted to talk about.

> She clinched her purse in her hands, continued to stare out the window, and nearly whispered, "Look . . . I never met you, I don't even know your name. But you are my enemy. I hate you and everybody connected to this school and any other school for what you are trying to do to my baby, my precious child." (p. 2)

Karen, feeling the mother's anger and her own fear, realized she needed to respond mother to mother. "You carry a lot of pain, don't you?" she asked. Karen explained that she recognized this pain, that it was the same anguish she had lived with as her own mother tried to deal with Karen's sister's learning difficulties. The mother, tears rolling down her cheeks, told Karen that her son had been dropped as an infant, that he had brain damage, that the doctors had told her first that he would not live and then that he would not walk or talk.

> Last year his school told me he needed special education. . . . It's the same story over and over. Nobody know what he can do. Just like the doctors didn't. . . . I didn't know 'til today they had made him repeat first grade. I came to tell *you*, teacher lady, he is never going to be in special education. . . . I am going to watch every move you make with him. . . . I do not want him sitting doing nothing; I want him learning. And just so you know, I don't care who I hurt to protect my child. (p. 3, emphasis in original)

"How would I have responded?" I asked myself, reading Hankins's account. Would I have shown my fear, backed out the door with empty promises, called the police to escort her out of my room? Would I have been angry, defensive, patronizing?

Action Opportunity: Talk about it. What would you have done if you were Karen? Are there parents at your school whom you are afraid of, whom you dread talking with, parents who have feelings of anger and hatred toward you or the school? Parents, are there teachers you feel this way about?

- Take 5 minutes to write about an uncomfortable situation between a parent and a teacher.
- Select two or three of these scenarios to role-play. It may be particularly effective if a parent takes a teacher role, and vice versa. Act out as accurately as possible the way the encounter actually occurred with coaching from the person who wrote about the incident.
- Next, two more volunteers start at the same point but act out another way the event might have evolved. If possible, have a third duo act out yet another possibility. Each enactment should be working toward empathy, respect, and a resolution that supports the parent, the teacher, and ultimately the child.
- Open the discussion to the different approaches and interaction in the various role-playing situations.

There are many ways to respond to Karen and the mother; your actions will be different based on your experiences and on the personalities and the dynamics of the particular situation.

I thought you might like to know what Karen did. Once again she drew on her own family to understand the mother who seemed to be threatening her. She told her more about her sister Kathy's brain damage, about schools that were not able or willing to teach her, about conferences with teachers and administrators that left the family devastated. She touched the mother's arm, looked her in the face, and said:

> I promise I will not neglect him. I promise I will protect him and teach him where he is and take him as far as he can go with me. I also promise you that I will not refer him for any testing or special services. He is *your* child. Help me know what you want me to do; we will work together. (Hankins, 2003, p. 3)

If you find that sharing stories of schooling is valuable, you might plan ways for more families, students, and other educators in the school to participate. You might invite parents (or whoever is most involved in the child's upbringing) and educators to dialogue about school experiences in one or more of the following ways.

1. *School open house* (usually right after school begins, often the first time parents and teachers meet). Wouldn't it be nice to set the tone for the year of two-way communication in each classroom? Telling stories of schooling might begin the evening.
2. *Parent–teacher chats*, invitations to talk on an adult-to-adult basis, unlike Parent–Teacher conferences, which focus on the child. These could be held in individual teachers' rooms if several parents from one classroom are interested; in a central place like the library if there are several teachers and parents across grade levels; or perhaps most effectively in a community center, business, or neighborhood place of worship. Ask parents where they'd like to meet.

The invitation to dialogue might go something like this: "I'll bet all of us have some good school memories and some bad ones. One of my best memories was when Mrs. Lovingood read *The Black Stallion* aloud to us in third grade; I can still picture that horse in my mind. One of my worst memories was when I got paddled for talking too much in the seventh grade. It was painful and humiliating; I am still angry with that teacher."

One strategy for tapping into those memories is to make a list of each year in school. You might start by sketching a picture of the buildings in which you went to school. You could label the rooms that stand out for you, with the grade, teacher's name, whatever you can remember. Start adding notes on the drawings about key incidents. For me that would include Miss Jenny's Nursery School (I hurt her feelings because she baked me a birthday cake and I didn't eat any), Miss Evanoff's second grade (I ran away), Mr. Burr's seventh-grade reading class (he humiliated a classmate by telling everyone his ITBS score), Miss Nelson's twelfth-grade English class (she made a list for me of books she thought I should read before college). Encourage everyone to tell, and perhaps write, about any incident that has a strong emotional connection, positive or negative.

CONSIDERING CULTURAL DIFFERENCES

As you plan dialogues, there are many cultural norms and practices to keep in mind, some of which you may be aware of, others more subtle.

- First, it's critical to have bilingual interpreters for these chats for any family that speaks a home language other than English. If the school doesn't have someone who can take this responsibility (or if several classrooms are meeting at the same time), you might enlist community members, social services, local churches (e.g., Spanish-speaking or Korean-speaking congregations), bilingual parents, or older children.
- Second, asking a parent or a teacher to "tell a story" about their experiences may be embraced or resisted, depending on cultural norms. A colleague who is working with a small group of Cherokee in North Carolina learned that asking an elder to "tell me a story about . . ." got a very negative reaction; too many "stories" have been stolen

---

Action Opportunity: If you are reading this book as a group of parents and teachers, take the time to share your own stories of schooling. People are usually most comfortable doing this first with just one other person. Pair up and interview each other, informally, about your school experiences. You might ask each other about favorite memories—best teachers, best school friends, best day in the classroom, best field trip, best school program. Start positive. Then move on to the less-pleasant memories. It's important to talk about them, even the painful ones, but don't push your partner if you can see that he or she doesn't want to go there.

from Native Americans and then told out of context. Many stories are told for cultural reasons. Likewise, Mary Louise Buley-Meissner (2002), who teaches Hmong students, learned that "many Hmong elders are not accustomed to being asked direct questions about themselves. Therefore, it is more respectful . . . simply to ask open-ended questions, such as 'When you recall your childhood, what do you remember the most?', rather than pointed questions about what they did or felt" (p. 326).

- Third, if you are wondering how to take into account the differing cultural norms in your school community, think about how you are going about planning the conversations. Is all the planning done by school folks? If you are like most schools, somebody heard about this book, you formed a committee or used your professional development committee, or (heaven forbid) somebody said you had to "do" this book. (If it's the latter, tell them, "JoBeth said we should read and talk about this book only if we are really interested in forming partnerships between school and families. It's important that we choose to read it.") Because this is a book for teacher–family–community discussions, teachers, parents, and community members should be involved in designing the discussions. In addition to parents themselves, teaching assistants or staff members who may be members of different cultural communities from the majority of teachers can provide excellent insights into planning for diverse families.

As tuned in as we may be to obvious cultural differences such as ethnicity, economic conditions, or language differences, we may not be sensitive to other aspects of culture. If our invitations are always to "moms and dads," we overlook families headed by grandparents, unrelated caregivers, or gay partners. If we talk only about grade levels and homeroom teachers, and assume that all students are in the same classes and learn pretty much the same way, we marginalize the parents of students receiving special services.

Teri Holbrook is the mother of two wonderful and talented daughters who learn differently: Jillian and Michaela. Teri's story (Holbrook, 2003) is one of how schooling has disrupted her family's home life and turned her into a liar:

At 12, in 6th grade and having dyslexia, Michaela struggles to read. Her homework history has been fraught with sobs, breakdowns, and storms. Five-minute tasks frequently took an hour; hourlong tasks took days. While her 16-year-old sister, labeled gifted since 1st grade, received homework assignments that had her mixing paints and poring over Picasso reproductions, Michaela, who actually loved Picasso and was fascinated by the transitions in his periods, more often than not brought home paper-and-pencil assignments or was instructed to read 30 minutes every day, which, depending on the book, could mean as little as three pages. As a result, we've learned to do homework collaboratively, to use passive-aggressiveness selectively, and to quietly broaden our definition of reading to encompass all kinds of visual/verbal texts. Oh, yes—and we've learned to lie. In our house, resisting homework has become a political act.

Our resistance didn't erupt full-blown; like most insurrections, it built gradually. When Michaela was in second grade, her teacher sent home a television log with a written letter to parents telling us that we were to help the children record the hours they spent watching television every week, with the goal of decreasing television time and increasing reading time. The next day after school, I approached the teacher and explained that since we were a family with learning disabilities, some of our "reading" took place via television. The teacher looked at me, her face skeptical.

"We mainly watch the Discovery and the History Channels," I said, speaking fast as I tried to convince her. "Michaela just soaks up the information. She learns so much watching TV, much more than she would reading books at this point." The books she could read, I said, were far below her intellectual level, and it was important that we kept her mind and heart engaged. "We read with her at least an hour every day," I hastened to add. "We want her to hear good literature, good writing. And she's in a program to help her read on her own. But we're not going to cut back on television. I'm sorry, but I just don't think we can participate in this project."

When Michaela didn't turn in her television log that week, the teacher sent another one home with a note reminding us to fill it out. That second log I "lost" by burying it under a bundle of Goodwill clothes in the car trunk. The teacher didn't bring up the log again, but from that time on, there was tension between us. I had taken the first step in becoming a problem parent.

By the end of that year, that step had become a march as time and time again I tried to domesticate the assignments that came home in Michaela's bookbag. No, she wasn't going to redo her writing homework because she hadn't followed the assigned topic; she had worked on it for two hours and it was the most sustained writing she had ever done. Let's celebrate her success, not punish her. No, she wasn't going to redo her papier mache globe for the third time to make it "neater." She was frustrated with it, she had worked on it for a week, and it was her own work, unlike the other students whose parents freely admitted they had done the assignment themselves to avoid a confrontation with the teacher. No, she wasn't going to do the worksheets over. They were filled out, she'd answered the questions, let's move on. No . . . I'm sorry . . . I wish we could . . . I'm sorryi'msorryreallyiam . . . But no. . . .

The irony was at the same time Jillian, safe within the county gifted program, rarely had homework. Children should be allowed to play, her teacher explained. They spent enough time hunched over books at school. After school they should be outside, letting their imaginations run wild, exploring nature, exercising their bodies, and learning about the world first hand. But those were the gifted kids. As we came to perceive over time, in the logic of the educational culture, students with learning disabilities needed to be stay hunched, controlled, learning about the world as it was refracted through the smudged lens of pencil and paper. (pp. 4–6)

This story of schooling is intense, personal, and carefully crafted. Yet in many ways it is no different from the stories many of us have to tell about our own schooling or our children's schooling.

USING THE PAST TO UNDERSTAND THE PRESENT

You may be thinking that although talking about memories is interesting, and although it may be useful in creating a stronger sense of community among faculty members and families, it is not directly related to your child, your student, right here, right now. Karen Hankins (2003) showed how teachers—and, even more powerfully, teachers and parents together—can examine family pasts to imagine new futures for children.

Hankins's dad, Billy, was from a poor mill worker's family—a "linthead," in the local derogatory taunt. He did not do well in school; he couldn't read, spell, or do more than basic math when he got to fourth grade. He didn't care much about school. All he wanted to do was to be at home, to make sure his mother didn't die; at age 7, he had watched his father die. He told Karen,

> But in the fourth grade, every day after lunch, Miss Walton asked someone to go to the map and show us some spot she'd not talked about before, a place we had never heard of even. I loved that part of school . . . We didn't have books or magazines at home, nothing to read . . . but [a] map thumbtacked to the wall. (Hankins, 2003, p. 92)

Then Karen's dad told her about the day he found a place on the map no one had ever heard of: the Firth of Forth. The children had laughed at him, thinking he'd misread it.

> Miss Walton came close to the map and looked. She put her arm around my shoulder and smiled real big. She said, "Billy has shown us the Firth of Forth, in Scotland. I've never noticed it on a map. How wonderful that you've shown us something new. I can't wait to read about it" . . . and she just went on and on acting like I said smart stuff all the time. . . . When that teacher smiled at me and thanked me for teaching her something I felt something in school I'd never felt before. A teacher believed in me. (Hankins, 2003, pp. 92–93)

Billy's entry point to academic learning was geography, and Miss Walton showed him that if he could read and spell Madagascar, he could read and spell anything. Because she believed in him, Billy became not only a learner, but also a social-studies teacher and eventually Dr. Bill Hale, who taught at the University of Georgia. But the teaching in this story does not stop with Billy. Karen used this family story to reach Tommy.

Tommy and Eric were best friends, and both nonreaders by midyear in first grade. Karen had been working with Eric's family, a middle-class European American family, in what she described as a "Mayo Clinic" aggressive treatment approach; it was unusual for a child of Eric's background to struggle so. But listening to her father's story of the Firth of Forth, Karen had a devastating realization. She had been "treating" Tommy's lack of progress "more as an allergy: awful to deal with but something some kids just have . . . sure that the solution to his nonreader status lay beyond my control" in what seemed to be his "chaotic" African American family (Hankins, 2003, p. 90).

At about the same time, Tommy's mother called Hankins to ask how Tommy was doing in school; she had been talking to Eric's mother. Karen shared her concerns. Tommy's mother asked what he had to do to "make his pass," and Karen said he needed someone at home to work with him half an hour daily, reading to him, listening to him read, and doing word cards. The mother said she worked evenings, but his sister could do this with him. Then she asked Karen to do one more thing. "You tell Tommy that if he don't learn to read he won't make his pass. Show him that he's behind and what books he have to learn to read before school gets out. It will mean more coming from you. You the teacher. He'll believe you" (p. 89). Karen wrote:

> I am bothered by Tommy's mother's call. There are things that weren't said. . . . We both understand that Tommy and Eric, so much alike, always viewed together, were treated differently. When the privileged White boy couldn't read, none of us could make sense of it. When the nonmainstream African American male couldn't read, no one was surprised. My indictment of his "failure" was aimed squarely at his home, the mom, the lack of parental participation, the lack of value placed on reading in that home. (p. 89)

She had been treating Tommy and his family as her father and his family had been viewed by the school and community; the failure of a mill worker's child was understandable, perhaps expected. She began the "aggressive" treatment that she and Tommy's mother had agreed upon. "Before I started talking [to Tommy], I had felt a little bit as though I was about to deliver news that his dog had died. . . . [But] he wanted to know what was required and was trying to cut through my message to the specifics" (p. 94). "My mama said what book I got to read to make my pass," he asked. Karen pulled books off the shelf that were considered end-of-first-grade level and said he'd need to be able to read books like that by June.

Did Tommy make his pass? Did Eric? I wouldn't dream of spoiling a riveting story by telling you the ending. As the kids say, "If you want to know what happened, read the rest of the book." I will say that when teachers, parents, and students share their stories, empathize, and work together toward a common goal, we can rewrite children's stories, replacing the "expected" endings with ones that inspire others to see children and families as partners.

We've focused primarily on one teacher in this chapter; we'll meet many other outstanding teachers and parents in other chapters. But isn't it amazing what one teacher, working together with families, can do? Of all the many elaborate ways we as educators have devised to "get parents involved," we may have overlooked one of the most important: sitting down together and sharing our stories.

CHAPTER 2

Writing Cultural Memoirs

Communion

You smelled of jasmine and wrote
on monogrammed stationery
and I wanted to grow up to be
like you. You taught me how to accept

or decline an invitation, to frost a
red velvet cake, to dispose of sanitary napkins,
and somewhere between Sunday school,
standing up straight, and not dragging

my feet you taught me about racism,
said that I would understand how you felt
about blacks if I ever worked with them,
that some people are black but don't act it,

and that only selfish people have biracial children
because these children will never fit in any place
and even in my middle-class isolation, and my
adolescent naiveté, I knew you were wrong.

Now my son rests on your silk lap
surrounded by pretense and perfume.
He laughs when you eat his fingers,
his voice a peal of small bells.

Are things still so black and white
for you? Do you think as you smile
that this Christ child should not
have come to us? You who ate pieces

of her own three, have your lips not noticed
that our boys taste more alike
than different? Close your eyes
and taste the body and the blood

that smiles at you now;
let this little holy one
bring to you a ray
of sweet redemption.

—May Jenkins

May—a teacher, a poet, a mother, a White woman married to a Black man—wrote this cultural-memoir poem about a close relative, about society, about how she became the person she is. Cultural memoirs can take many forms, but at heart they are all detective stories; they are all journey pieces; they are all social commentary.

Who am I as a cultural being, and what are the influences in my life that have made me who I am? This is a question I ask people to consider in some of my classes for teachers and those studying to become teachers. We engage in a process of exploring this question and write our cultural memoirs. This process is often one of the most important ways we have of reflecting not only on our own cultures, but also on our students' cultures, and how our different as well as shared cultural backgrounds influence our classroom relationships. My students then guide their elementary students in the process of researching and writing cultural memoirs. The most important part is weaving these two memoir experiences together as they reflect on these questions: How has exploring my cultural influences helped me think about the cultural influences of my students? How does that new understanding of myself and of my students help me form stronger relationships that build on the cultural resources my children bring to the classroom?

In this chapter we explore various processes of writing cultural memoirs and hope that you'll find a way to modify the process for yourself and for your children and students.

READING CULTURAL MEMOIRS

Writing cultural memoirs provides the wonderful and necessary excuse to read them. Maybe you can start a "Memoir" section in the professional library at your school for family members as well as school folk to check out. I keep a shelf of these in my office and have loaned them to students, custodians, faculty members, secretaries, and teachers. One of the best conversations I've had in 20 years as a professor at the University of Georgia was with Sarah, a custodian in my building who borrowed Dorothy Allison's (1992) *Bastard Out of Carolina*. She returned it with an apology for keeping it so long. "I read some parts over and over. This is my life, right here in this book." Then she told me about her life, and it was like the book. Like the central character, Bone, she had been abused, and like Bone she had found a way to stop the abuse.

What makes something a *cultural* memoir? I like Geneva Gay's (2000) definition of culture as "a dynamic system of social values, cognitive codes, behavioral standards, worldviews, and beliefs used to give order and meaning to our own lives as well as the lives of others. . . . Culture determines how we think, believe, and behave . . . and how we teach and learn" (pp. 8–9). Most memoirs are, at least in part, cultural memoirs in that the authors examine some portion of their lives through one or more cultural lenses. They are deeply contextualized in time and place, as well as in social and political issues. Cultural "memoirs" may be short stories, essays, or even poems; these shorter forms are a great place for a group to start because you can read them together—no homework! If these forms lead you to book-length memoirs, here are some of my favorites.

While Rick Bragg's (1997) *All Over But the Shoutin'* does tell the story of how he became an award-winning journalist, the cultural lens of the book focuses on growing up in the generational poverty of Alabama that could have easily buried him. James McBride (1996) focused on race, and to a lesser degree religion, as he told two tales in *The Color of Water: A Black Man's Tribute to His White Mother*. His own memoir alternates with his mother's as she recounted leaving her conservative, White, Jewish family to live in an African American Christian community. Other delightful, poignant, and/or painful memoirs are Anne Lamott's (1999) "sobering" account of overcoming addiction and finding grace in *Traveling Mercies* and Anchee Min's (1994) harrowing and triumphant journey through the Chinese cultural revolution in *Red Azalea*. Who could be unmoved by Richard Rodriguez (1982) when he described his Mexican father trying to say the familiar blessing over dinner in the unfamiliar English tongue and his children laughing at him in *Hunger of Memory*? Concha Delgado-Gaitan (2001), whose work I refer to often in this book, included a cultural memoir in the final chapter of *The Power of Community: Mobilizing for Family and Schooling*; this and other teacher memoirs may be particularly interesting. Many groups enjoy starting with Sandra Cisneros's (1989) *The House on Mango Street* about growing up Latina in Chicago because each chapter is a short, beautifully crafted jewel of memory. She provides jumping-off points for us as writers (for example, describing the members of her family by their hair or telling "best friend" stories).

As you read other people's memoirs, you'll begin writing your own—in your head, at least. To make the leap to print, buy a notebook or journal that will make you *want* to write because you love the cover, or appreciate the wide lines, or can carry it easily in your pocket or purse. If you are like me, you may write best at the computer. So start a folder; put it on your computer desktop so you see it every day; color-code it your favorite color; and scan or drag some of your favorite family pictures into the folder.

GATHERING PHOTOGRAPHS

Photographs are a gold mine. My students love the class session when they can bring in photographs and talk about their lives. Your kids will too, especially if you have cameras they can take home to document their lives or encourage those who do not have photographs to draw their own "photo." But that's all in another chapter—for now, we are focusing on adults. So here are some strategies: Gather pictures from different periods in your life. Go through those boxes, albums, and iPhoto files, asking yourself, "What were my cultural influences?"

It may help to think in terms of some common as well as some more invisible cultural categories: race, social class, gender, ethnicity, geographic region, religion, nationality, language/dialect, sexual orientation, schooling, physical or mental health or ability, and family structure. Think about these categories in terms of what has shaped your values, beliefs, and sense of yourself. My students sometimes say that they don't have a culture— "I'm just a plain girl who was born in America, and basically that's it!" one told me. As she thought and wrote more about it, she realized that by being a White, middle-class, Baptist, heterosexual, Southern female she was indeed part of a culture and that she had many powerful influences from home, church, and school. We all have practices, beliefs, and attitudes about each of the categories above, whether we are in the majority, the minority, or some more hybrid place.

As you think about your cultural influences, take new pictures. If you can, go back to some of the places you have lived. Photograph the places you played, worshipped, sneaked cigarettes, went to school, met your first love, and rode bikes with your best friend. Photograph things that you may not know the significance of yet but to which you have a strong reaction. Photograph parts of town that were not part of your life. Someday I will go to Breckenridge, Texas, and photograph the "colored" school, if it is still standing. I went to school from first to fifth grade in that town and never knew I attended a segregated school. I'll go to Hill City, Kansas, and ask whether I can photograph the home in the nearby freedman-settlement of Nichodemus where Ms. Letha Napue lived; she cleaned our house, babysat for us, and ended up being my mom's one enduring friend and eventual correspondent when we moved, and I visited her only once. In Lawrence, Kansas, I'll take pictures of the First United Methodist Church and look in the phone book to find out what religions co-existed with mine in a town I called home for 18 years.

Where will you go? A middle-school teacher in the Red Clay Writing Project recently wrote a poetic cultural memoir, shaping it as a conversation with a tree. That tree had been her only friend and confidante in a childhood marked by dissent and desertion. She had never written about those years, finding it too painful, too personal, and something of a betrayal of her mother. But she took a picture of that tree, and it all began spilling out. She wrote, cried, blamed, forgave, and thanked the tree for being there for her all those years.

TALKING ABOUT CULTURAL INFLUENCES

There are several next steps. You might arrange the photographs in some thematic or chronological or emotional-impact order; tape them into your journal (or scan them into your computer); and start jotting or webbing or drafting picture by picture. You might select one—perhaps you had your "tree"—and write everything from that one picture. You might put the pictures away and just begin writing, creating cultural images that no photograph could capture. One of the most effective ways is to talk with someone else about the photographs.

It is often helpful to have two different kinds of conversations. The first is with people you know well, family members and friends, who shared the life experiences in the photos with you—"Hey, Mom, I was looking at this picture of Grandpa, and it made me think of a story he told me about the Osage Indians in his town when I was little, and now that I'm older, I'm thinking about it in a new way. Do you remember him talking about that?" or "Lew, do you remember Billy Anderson? There he is in this photo of our high school band, playing snare drum. I know now that he was gay; what did we think then? When we were dating, did we even think about how it was we were attracted to each other and not to someone who was our own gender?" It is fascinating talking with people who lived such experiences with you; I've often learned that I have a different memory from someone I thought had lived the same event.

The other kind of conversation is with someone who did not live these experiences with you. So the second part is perfect for your study group. Divide into partners—maybe parent and teacher, maybe younger generation and older generation, maybe just the person you are sitting by. Give each person in your pair 10–15 minutes to talk about his or her picture(s). Let's say a parent, Mr. Singh, and a teacher, Ms. Bailey-Jones, are interviewing each other. Mr. Singh asks Ms. Bailey-Jones to talk about her pictures and takes notes as she talks. He's not writing down everything but is capturing big ideas, strong emotions, and especially phrases that strike him as important: "We were never allowed . . .", "Dad was surprised when . . .", "We just didn't talk about . . .", for example. At the end of 10–15 minutes, Mr. Singh gives Ms. Bailey-Jones the notes so she'll have a place to start writing, and they switch roles. Here are some questions that might be helpful:

- Tell me about these pictures.
- Which picture evokes the strongest emotional memory?
- What were the attitudes about (religion, race, Northerners, people living in this part of town) in your family?
- Tell me more about your high school years. What was the culture of your school?
- Who or what is missing from this/these photograph(s)?
- If you stepped into this photograph now, at your age, how would things be different? What would you say or think or do?
- Your family seems very close. How do you think your (mom, aunt, grandpa) shaped you? Was it by example, stories, lectures, or something else?
- What was going on in the country that influenced you during these (high school, military service, college) years?

These conversations may lead you to hunt down other resources. Doesn't your mom have newspaper clippings from all your years on the soccer team? Is there a teacher, rabbi, or buddy from junior high you might talk with? The library might have your hometown newspaper on file in some digital form.

My students who were preparing to become teachers learned a lot about themselves and their cultural influences from talking and writing about the photographs they chose. For example:

> Ladonna's picture of herself with her mother at high school graduation generated a reflection on her mother's early marriage, her failure to finish high school, and how that regret led her to push her children to excel in school. Cassy's pictures were of a series of buildings: the house where she was born, the one filled with "the fighting, the screaming, and the crying"; her grandparents' farm, where she and her mom lived after the divorce; the school where she faced "the scariest moment of my life" as a new student and learned to be "courageous." Amanda included a picture of herself in a band uniform and wrote, "Son, I want you to know how much music means to me and how that has shaped my culture. The day I was born, Papa played the guitar and sang me a song in the hospital—'Amanda' by Waylon Jennings. I was named after a country song—as were your aunts Aimee and Jolene." (Allen & Labbo, 2001, p. 43)

WRITING AND SHARING CULTURAL MEMOIRS

Your cultural memoir may be one poem or vignette written in one sitting (do take time in your study group to actually write), or it may become a lifelong project. If you decide to invest more than an afternoon, think about what form your writing might take. You could make an iMovie as you talk about your old neighborhood, school, or afternoons at the Boys or Girls Club. You might write a children's book, as one teacher did to share with her students the "culture of divorce" in which she grew up. Her students asked to read it over and over; several then wrote thoughtful pieces about their own family structures. Another teacher made an alphabet book of his life, complete with action shots of himself in the outdoor culture he loved. Several teachers have written letters to their children—born and unborn—about their lives. Other genres include poetry; short stories; and multigenre pieces in which teachers include fiction, letters, poetry, wedding announcements, telegrams, photographs, and even obituaries (real or fictitious).

The most fun and potentially most valuable part of writing cultural memoirs is sharing and discussing them. Read them with young people at home and in school, and show them how to research and write their own. Read them with family members, who will all want copies. Most important, read them together in your school community—teachers, counselors and other support faculty members, family members, students, custodians, office staff, principals. Make it a family literacy event. But most of all, give yourselves time in your study group to talk about the issues and perspectives in your memoirs.

Kacie, an undergraduate preparing to become a middle-school teacher, struggled to find a focus for her cultural memoir. By talking with others in my class, many of them already teachers, she began to see that there was an unexamined aspect of her "safe, loving, sheltered" childhood that she needed to explore before she returned to her hometown to teach. She was from a town that experienced a rapid influx of Hispanic families in a short period of time, giving a boost to the economy and a challenge to the schools and many residents. Kacie wrote her cultural memoir in the third person:

> Once upon a time there lived a little girl. This little girl lived in Dalton: "The Carpet Capital of the World!" Dalton is a great place to grow up; it is a friendly, prosperous town. . . . When the little girl started school, she noticed she had many children in her class who never talked to her . . . she asked her mom why . . . and her mom explained that they were from Mexico and they couldn't speak English. She told the little girl that their parents moved to Dalton to work and try to make a better life for their family. . . .
>
> When the girl started junior high, many of the Hispanic boys threatened other students with weapons at school, and some of the girls would pick fights. . . . Gang symbols were spray painted all over school property. . . . The girl and her friends didn't feel safe. . . . In high school . . . the girl heard her teachers talking about how the Hispanic students used their poor English as an excuse not to have to do their work. They just passed them onto the next grade because the majority of them would drop out when they reached 16 and got a job in a carpet mill. This seemed very unfair to the girl. She worked hard to get good grades while these other students just sat there and did nothing, and yet they passed every class.
>
> [Her] last year of high school, the girl became very good friends with one of her Hispanic classmates and began to feel guilty for the way she felt toward the Hispanics in general. With each comment that would automatically enter her mind, she felt like she was betraying her friend. This made the girl realize how unfairly she was stereotyping. . . .
>
> Today, the girl still struggles to erase the stereotypes she has grown up with for the past 22 years. It is so hard to ignore the fears, beliefs, and memories that have been building since kindergarten. But

by recognizing the root of those stereotypes, the girl is more aware of why she has felt differently toward this group of people. . . .

Kacie knew she had done very important work, but she was hesitant to read it to the class when we met at my house the last night to share our memoirs. "I didn't want my classmates to be offended or think I was racist," she wrote to me. But she did share and found much support from other members of the class, both prospective and experienced teachers. They applauded her honesty and reinforced her belief that she had to confront and overcome her stereotypes to be an effective teacher of all children—Hispanic as well as Anglo.

Your cultural-memoir process will serve as a reflective foundation for reading and pondering the rest of this book, whether that is with an actual or "virtual" study group, in a class, or on your own. We'll be considering connections between reflection on your own cultural influences and what it means to form meaningful relationships with families from a variety of cultural heritages. Even if all the students and teachers in your school are African American, for example, you have different cultural influences related to when you grew up, where you lived previously, who raised you, and a myriad of other influences. Sharing cultural memoirs is a way of looking past the "surface homogeneity" to differences that make a difference and commonalities that make a community.

VARIATIONS ON CULTURAL MEMOIRS

Drawing neighborhood maps led a group of Los Angeles teachers to uncover or recover cultural treasures from their childhoods (Frank, 2003). The teachers, led by Carolyn Frank in a graduate course, each drew an annotated map of the neighborhood, a drawing/writing activity that has been used widely in the National Writing Project. These "memory maps" included dwellings, stores, creeks, animals, and other landmarks, with annotations such as "Judy's horses" and "St. Agnes school and church" (Frank, p. 189). Teachers talked as they drew, telling each other about places, events, and family members from their childhoods in China, Taiwan, Vietnam, Mexico, and Los Angeles. The oral stories became written ones that they read to one another. One teacher wrote

I have six siblings, and whenever I tell people that I have four elder sisters and two younger brothers, their faces always fill with surprise. . . . The reason is that in our Chinese tradition . . . we need to have boys to carry on the family

name and business. . . . When I was born, my grandfather was very disap-
pointed because I was a girl. He gave me a very boyish name, hoping that I
would in turn bring the luck of boy with my mother's next baby. (p. 188)

What would your maps of childhood neighborhoods remind you of?
Maybe your parents didn't have five girls just to get a male heir. But as
you draw your neighborhood, are there any messages inscribed on the side-
walks, the apartment walls, the sandlot baseball diamond, or the school
desks about being a girl or being a boy? Who in your neighborhood did
what jobs? What did your teachers tell you, directly or indirectly, about
what you could or couldn't, should or shouldn't do? Were the expectations
in your family the same for all children regarding classes, extracurricular
activities, careers, and higher education?

Other stories evoked by mapping their neighborhoods described the
difficult transitions some teachers had faced as children when their families moved to the United States. Samantha, whose mother was Chinese and
father Vietnamese, told of her move to California when she was in fourth
grade.

> One day, two of my male classmates came to visit. I . . . was in my "at home"
> clothes which were light blue Chinese pajamas . . . .[T]his is what all the kids
> wore in my homeland. . . . One of the guys (who was also Chinese) gave me a
> look and said that I shouldn't be wearing that kind of outfit out in public. I asked
> why. He replied that we were in America now and that we should dress like
> other Americans. . . . From then on, I became overly sensitive and self-conscious
> about myself, even my culture. I stopped wearing pajamas out on the street
> and even went so far as to not speak my native language out on the streets or
> at school. What I learned from my classmate's comment was that if I wanted to
> fit in and not be an embarrassment, I had to be like everyone else in dress as
> well as in speech. That incident taught me a lot about what I had to do to fit in,
> but on the other hand, I also lost a lot. (Frank, 2003, pp. 189–190).

Because Samantha told this story—this cultural memoir—I have no
doubt that she will be better able to relate to the students she teaches who
feel alienated, self-conscious, or even ashamed of some aspect of their cultural heritage. Maybe she will help them draw maps and write memories.

These neighborhood maps and childhood stories may very well become
stories of schooling, as we explored in the previous chapter. Mariana, another teacher in Frank's class, had entered elementary school in the United
States speaking no English; Mariana's teachers spoke no Spanish:

> I don't remember my teachers ever reading to me. I don't remember them
> showing me how to add or subtract. I don't even remember the teacher speak-
> ing to me. I was invisible . . . it has been 22 years and this experience still

haunts me . . . it brings tremendous sadness to my heart as I recall the shame
and worthlessness I felt. (p. 190)

How important it is for us as teachers and parents to use our maps to un-
earth those painful times in our childhoods—the very ones we've so carefully buried. No child will ever be invisible in Mariana's classroom. And
perhaps by sharing her story with others, Mariana will also be able to dis-
solve some of the sadness in her heart.

In another variation of writing cultural memoir, Linda Winston (1997)
described a process she called "cultural autobiography." With a small
group of teachers, Winston shared Kathryn Morgan's stories of her great-
grandmother, Caddy, who had been a slave. In *Children of Strangers: The
Stories of a Black Family* (1981), Morgan wrote about how these stories guided
and inspired her family through four generations. Winston's group collected and shared their own family stories. Who are the storytellers in your
family? What are the taken-for-granted treasures, the tales that get told
whenever your family gathers, the lessons passed on from generation to
generation?

My husband, Lew, was the bedtime storyteller for our three children,
sometimes reading favorite books but more often telling stories of his childhood. The children loved to hear about the day the can of corn fell on his
nose; the time he threw his brother's favorite cap out of the window on a
steep mountain in Colorado; and his dogs "Forty Four" and "Seventy,"
named after the Kansas highways on which they'd been rescued. He told
them about summers on his grandparents' farm in southeast Kansas: riding
the propane tank "horse," running to the cellar when the sky blackened,
and watching from the barn as a chicken fence they'd worked all morning
to install was blown to splinters by a tornado. Lew also invented countless
stories of the Bubble Gum Kids. What grand adventures they had, floating
above oceans, mountains, and their own neighborhoods and schoolyards
in the giant bubble they blew in each installment. Last night, our grandchildren Luke and Grace begged Grandpa, "Tell us another Bubble Gum
Kids story—one you told our mom when she was a little girl!" Like giant
bubble-gum bubbles, family stories are powerful vehicles.

This chapter opened with a cultural memoir in poetic form. I love engaging with groups of teachers in writing poetry that help capture the critical incidents, repeated messages, or buried memories that shaped us as
cultural beings. George Ella Lyon's poem, "Where I'm From," is a wonderful catalyst and "mentor poem" for adults as well as young people. It
begins, "I am from clothespins/from Clorox and carbon tetra-chloride/I
am from dirt under the back porch . . ." My favorite lines are "I'm from He
restoreth my soul/with a cottonball lamb/and ten verses I can say myself."

Lyon's (1999) poetry workshop book suggests a process for writing "Where I'm From" poems. Linda Christensen (2000) uses "Where I'm From," praise poems, "Remember Me," and forgiveness poems to help her high school students reflect on their lives through poetry. Teachers have found these forms to be wonderful prompts for their own memories. "I Am" poems can be an even more direct way of reflecting on how we are becoming who we are. I often share a powerful version by Shuaib Meacham (2003), which begins

> I Am
> Descended from runaway slaves
> Guided by stars in the darkness
> Tiny like letters on a page
> Illegal to decipher—risking graves
> By violating prohibitions against reading instruction
> Like Frederick Douglass teaching forty in hiding
> They still think we don't want to read . . .

Action Opportunity: In small groups of parents, children, and teachers together, draw maps of your childhood neighborhood (some of us have lots of them; it will be interesting to see which one you choose). Label them as you would have at that time—in your home language, neighborhood slang, or child perception. Share the maps in your group, talking about particularly vivid memories associated with specific places on the map. Using the map, tell or write one or more stories from your reflections—or create one or more "Where I'm From," "I Am," "remember me," praise, or forgiveness poem.

This is also an action that can be done by teachers and children in school and by children with their parents at home. Good books to help children think about their neighborhood maps are *My Map Book* (Fanelli, 2001), which includes childlike maps, and *Madlenka* (Sis, 200), in which a young girl visits diverse neighbors on one city block. Older students might do this activity in connection with a study of maps, geographical regions, cultural heritage, or biography and memoir with their parents. You might create a class book, iMovie, or PowerPoint presentation of *Stories from the Neighborhood* that includes student, parent, and teacher stories; families will flock to a classroom or neighborhood center to get the book, view the movie, and hear their children read.

REFLECTING ON OUR CULTURAL INFLUENCES

It is not always an easy thing, thinking about the people dearest to us.

Grandpa Paine was my hero. He thought his grandchildren were the most remarkable students, pianists, writers, and artists he had ever known. He had us bring our report cards every time we visited. Then he would take me downtown to the hotel where he had coffee with his friends every day (my brothers must have gone too, but I don't remember them). He always wore a suit and a hat, and seemed to me the most distinguished man I had ever met. He proudly introduced me to his friends, passed my report card around for their feigned astonishment, and asked me to perform my latest piano pieces. He made me feel like the most special person in the world.

Grandpa Paine left a written legacy of my cultural history in a letter he wrote me in 1964 to help with a high school assignment to write my autobiography. I have read the letter so many times throughout my life—to sort out the Confederates from the Yankees; to recall a famous "Paine" connection, however tenuous. But mostly I read it to remember Grandpa, his wit, humor, and overflowing love for his grandchildren. If Grandpa was my hero, his hero was his own Grandpa Paine. In his letter to me, Grandpa wrote:

> Back in 1880 Grandpa Paine secured the grazing rights on the Sac and Fox nation, which later became Oklahoma Territory. By treaty he agreed to furnish the Sac and Fox Indians with the beef which was due them from the U.S. government and in return owned ranching rights on a region which extended roughly from Stroud to Stillwater to Tulsa. . . . When the state was opened for settlement Grandpa "homesteaded" the land. . . . In 1922 he secured the mahogany lumber concession in Gold Coast West Africa. . . . He went there when he was 64 Years old and there were only six other white people in the entire colony.

Grandpa went on to tell me that his Grandpa Paine made a fortune traveling to the Gold Coast of Africa, where he helped "develop" the gold and mahogany trade there. He also wrote proudly that the Paines were among the White settlers of Oklahoma and made fortunes from the gas and oil resources. We are in a large part the stories we tell, and Grandpa told us over and over of the young Indian woman he had befriended, hired to work for him, and helped enter the local community college. She quit work and dropped out of college—I never heard why—but he used this as an example of how "they" just didn't value education and hard work the way "we" do.

Finally, at 50, I read this beloved letter with fresh eyes, eyes that at once looked more closely and stepped back to read the social, cultural, and political context of Grandpa's proud recounting. Other stories crowded Grandpa's, voices I couldn't ignore, like Dennis McAuliff's (1994) investigation of his grandmother's murder in *The Deaths of Sybil Bolton: An American History*. This history was part of my family's history, taking place in the same part of Oklahoma during the "Osage Reign of Terror"—a systematic killing spree by White men in the 1920s for the oil rights and ensuing wealth the Osage held. When Grandpa talked with pride about his grandfather's huge ranch and grazing rights, he did not talk about the people those lands had been stolen from. He did not talk about the exclusion of Indians when the Oklahoma Territory "was opened" or the record of broken promises to the Indians. Was his "treaty" one of them or only a cruelly ironic arrangement to give back a small portion of something that originally belonged to the real "settlers"? Neither did he make a connection between his own fortunes from the natural gas and oil resources and the Osage Reign of Terror.

And Great-Great-Grandfather Paine's heroic exploits in Africa—were they actually exploitations? The lucrative mahogany trade did not benefit Ghana, which now suffers the effects of deforestation. Entrepreneurs like Great-Great-Grandpa Paine didn't seem to question their right to make their fortunes, either in Ghana or Oklahoma. More troubling, neither did my grandfather, one of the most kind and fair people I have ever known. Neither did I, until I began writing my cultural memoir.

The whole process of cultural memoiring is a way for us to examine our own histories with thoughtful adult eyes, to learn about ourselves in an intentional way, perhaps even to examine our unexamined privileges in society. But it is not a self-centered "All About Me" piece of writing. It is an exploration on behalf of our children, our students, as much as for ourselves. If we don't know what shaped and continues to shape us, how can we be as sensitive and insightful and reflective as we need to be to shape the lives of our young people?

We'll conclude this chapter with the most powerful letter I ever received from a student. Susan, a White, middle-class, twentysomething woman, had written in her cultural memoir early in the semester, "I am who I am because of the normal everyday routine that my family goes through without giving it a second thought." Through work in a culturally diverse school setting, reading the work of educators who prompted her to think differently about culture and families, and being asked to reflect on the relationship between her cultural influences and those of the children she would soon be teaching, Susan eventually gave it a second thought (Allen & Labbo, 2001).

> As you can imagine, this is somewhat of a difficult letter for me to write. Please . . . don't think any less of me after you read it. . . . My parents are not obviously racist people. They do not sit around and talk about niggers or chinks or spics or anything like that. . . . I don't think that anyone told me to dislike black people, but I was raised that I was better.
>
> Our maid is black. Our yardman is black. The trashmen on our street are black. The janitors and cooks at my school are black. . . . The man at the bank is white. My teachers are white. My doctor is white. . . . My parents' friends are white. Are the black people bad people? No. Do I want their jobs? No. I was never told that blacks are inferior, but the ones that I came in contact with had jobs and lives that I did not want. . . . I did not have a positive black role model to look up to, so I assumed that white people were better. . . . I saw who were members of the Country Club and who were waiters. I saw who were teachers and who were janitors. . . . No one showed me on purpose, it was right there in front of me. And then I went to school.
>
> I went to a private school through second grade. Then I switched to a public school until seventh. There were black people there and they were very kind, friendly people. We all got along well, with no problems. I did not think any less of them, but did I have them to spend the night? Of course not. . . . It wasn't my parents that didn't allow me to have them over, I just don't think I considered it. They were school friends and that is where it ended. But, I think it had to have been mutual, because I was never invited to their house either. Again, no one told me I was better, I saw it. The white children had better grades. The white mothers volunteered at the school. The teachers were white. The principal was white. And the lunch ladies were black. . . .
>
> At my high school, white people were the minority. . . . The blacks drove "hoopties," blasted rap, were in gangs, and caused trouble. . . . They were all in the lower level classes. It was 90% white in the 300 level and AP classes. I mainly came in contact with the troublemakers in homeroom. I did not see them in my classes. They were not in the clubs that I was in. They were not on yearbook staff. . . . The classes I was in were almost like being in a private school all over again. . . . There were [some black people in my classes] and they were good students from nice families. There were white people in the lower classes that caused trouble, too. I convinced myself that there was a difference between black people and niggers, just like there is a difference between white people and white trash. . . . The blacks in my classes were better. We, the upperlevel students, were better.
>
> I cannot tell you when all of this changed. . . . It may have been when I had my first placement in a school. It may have been when I was reading

articles for classes. It may have been repeatedly listening to people blanketly refer to all black people as niggers. Regardless, something snapped. I could no longer take it. . . . I figured out how unfair it is to have a class of mixed ethnicities, mixed cultures, mixed socioeconomic classes and for me to think that I, and everyone like me, is better. What makes me better? Because I have had more opportunities, more privileges, I am better? Because my dad made more money, I am better? . . . That makes no sense. What is better about me than these children whose parents work their tails off to give their children clothes and food? . . . Because we never really struggled, I am better? That makes no sense. It makes no sense. . . .

I cannot continue to think that I am better if I want to be a successful teacher or citizen. How could my class be fair? . . . If I had ideas that they weren't as good as I am or the other children are, it would eventually become a self-fulfilling prophecy. . . .

[S]o let me assure you of one thing. This has changed and is continuing to change daily. I have realized how detrimental this could potentially be. . . . I know that one cannot teach with preconceived notions. One cannot lead a class if they think that some cannot be as good or as smart as others are. What if I had never figured this out? How many kids would've suffered through my class? It terrifies me to think about it. The good news is that I have, and please do not think less of me for having to undertake this journey through self evaluation. At least I did. (pp. 51–52)

Like Susan, we have all grown up with cultural blinders. Sharing cultural memoirs—oral or written—gives each of us an opportunity to explore what we have missed because of those blinders, and what difference it might make in coming together as a diverse school community to see our cultural influences through fresh eyes.

CHAPTER 3

Learning With and From Families

"I feel so sorry for that poor child. Charlene's so-called 'family' life is chaos. That family has nothing—I mean nothing—they have been homeless off and on for the last three years, Mom can't hold a job, who even knows where Dad is."

"I know the family—I had Rico's older brothers—don't expect anything from his parents. They never came to school once, and you can't reach them by phone because they get their service cut off about every other month."

"Where do I start with a child like J'Mario? He has no language."

Have you ever heard statements like these? Have you ever felt that undertone, even when teachers have genuine sympathy for the children they teach, that it's really kind of hopeless, given their home situation? I have heard variations of these comments for 30 years, from my days teaching in Head Start and Follow Through to my conversations with preservice teachers shocked by their first practicum experiences.

One particularly vivid example from my experience illustrates how a child can be doomed to failure. In a study of children we "worried about," Jeremiah's teachers and I followed him from first through third grade (Allen, Michalove, & Shockley, 1993). He struggled his first two years, needing constant attention from teachers and classmates, but had finally begun to blossom as a reader, writer, and a child learning to get along with others. However, Ms. Gilcrest, his teacher in third grade, had little patience for his struggles and laid them firmly at the door of his family. In October she noted:

> Jeremiah is having a really hard time in third grade, mostly because of his behavior. . . . I send home weekly notes for the parents. At first Jeremiah's were signed by his grandmother, but none of the rest have come back. . . . In one I even asked his mom to call me. I didn't realize they had no phone. He spends his weekends with his dad, but most of the time I think he's with his grandmother. His dad and mother or grandmother, I don't know which, both came to open house. . . . (pp. 96–97)

In March, Ms. Gilcrest saw some improvement but confided, "He rarely has his homework done. Last week his mother signed his homework, but it was all done incorrectly." During her June interview, she reported:

> Jeremiah will repeat third grade—he just isn't making it. . . . He is really struggling with decoding and comprehension. Some of the decoding problems fit the pattern of his language—he slurred his words and left off endings. I think he had few role models at home who spoke clearly. . . . I felt it would be an injustice to put him in fourth grade, that it would be unfair to him. I can't say I feel bad. He just wasn't convinced he needed to do the work. And there was no response from home for a conference about the problems. He didn't say much about it. . . . But one day he wrote in his journal, "I've been thinking about what my mama told me, that I'm going to fail third grade. It made me cry and cry and cry." (pp. 97–98)

Jeremiah and his family failed this teacher's expectations for family structure, parental involvement, even acceptable language usage. He failed third grade, his second "failure" in four years of school, increasing the likelihood that he would not graduate from high school to almost 90%.

Ms. Gilcrest accepted her responsibility to teach Jeremiah. She tried different special services and classroom strategies, but she did not know how to engage family members she viewed as more of a hindrance to his education than as a potential support.

Action Opportunity: Teachers, who are your Jeremiahs? Who are the students who have struggled the most in your classrooms? Who are their parents/families? Make a list of everything you know about the family. Parents, who are your Ms. Gilcrests? Who are the teachers who didn't seem to value—or even much like—you or your family? Make a list of everything you know about that teacher. Do not read the lists! We'll come back to Jeremiah and Ms. Gilcrest.

Shifting our thinking away from deficits—a teacher who doesn't like my child, a mother who can't correct third grade homework—and learning more about strengths and connections is the focus of this chapter. How can learning about families and their strengths lead to more culturally relevant teaching? What do families know, and how can schools build on that knowledge? What are my family resources, and how can I share them with my children's teachers? How can we, together, support student learning by dialogue between home and school that is built on mutual respect?

CULTURALLY RELEVANT TEACHING

The prophetic African American educator Carter G. Woodson, author of *The Mis-Education of the Negro* (1933/2005), recounted a remarkable story of culturally relevant education in the early 1900s. Following the U.S. imperialistic conquest of the Philippines, the U.S. government set out to "educate" the Filipinos. Woodson recounted:

> Numbers of "highly trained" Americans were carried there to do the work they entered upon their task by teaching the Filipinos just as they had taught American children. . . . The result was failure. Men trained at institutions like Harvard, Yale, Columbia, and Chicago could not reach these people and had to be dismissed from the service. . . .
>
> In the meantime, however, there came along an insurance man, who went to the Philippines to engage in business. He had never taught at all . . . but he understood people. . . . He filled the schoolroom with thousands of objects from the pupil's environment. In the beginning he did not use books very much, because those supplied were not adapted to the needs of the children. He talked about the objects around them. . . . In teaching the Filipinos music he did not sing "Come Shake the Apple-Tree." They had never seen such an object. He taught them to sing "Come Shake the Lomboy Tree," something which they had actually done. In reading he did not concentrate on the story of how George Washington always told the truth. They had never heard of

him and could not have appreciated that myth. . . . This real educator taught them about their own hero, José Rizal, who gave his life as a martyr for the freedom of his country. . . . The result, then, was that this man and others who saw the situation as he did succeeded. . . . (pp. 98–99)

The man Woodson described engaged in what Gloria Ladson-Billings called "culturally relevant teaching"—he learned the culture before trying to teach in it. In her must-read book, *The Dreamkeepers: Successful Teachers of African American Children* (1994), Ladson-Billings illustrated the tenets of culturally relevant teaching based on her in-depth study of eight effective teachers of African American children. While these teachers, five Black and three White, employed widely varied instructional programs and philosophies, they shared a deep understanding of and respect for African American children and their families in the urban schools in which they taught. The key was knowing the children's family cultures through ongoing, meaningful involvement in their communities in order that "students' real-life experiences are legitimized as they become part of the 'official curriculum'" (p. 117). Ladson-Billings described teachers who led Girl Scout troops, invited students to their homes for dinner, invited them over to play with their own children, invited small "lunch bunch" groups to eat with them in the classroom once a week, and attended student out-of-school sporting and musical events; one even invited children to Sunday breakfast and church with her if their parents called to approve. These culturally relevant teachers had close relationships not only with their students, but also with the students' families and communities.

Woodson (1933/2005) realized 70 years ago what Ladson-Billings so carefully detailed more recently. Interestingly, both asked whether African American children would be better served in separate schools and reached similar conclusions: "The emphasis is not upon the necessity for separate systems but upon the need for . . . schools and teachers who understand and continue in sympathy with those whom they instruct" (p. 18).

The critical question is this: How do we as educators come to understand and develop empathy for children and families whose cultural influences are different from our own? How do we as parents and teachers share our home cultures?

FAMILY FUNDS OF KNOWLEDGE

The concept of family funds of knowledge has influenced my thinking about connecting schools and homes more than perhaps any other educational effort. The work began in Tucson, Arizona, with a group of teachers and anthropology and education professors (Moll, Amanti, Neff, & Gonzáles, 1992); they have successfully challenged the deficit model of families and children and given us a powerful alternative. Their latest book, *Funds of Knowledge: Theorizing Practices in Households, Communities, and Classrooms* (Gonzáles, Moll, & Amanti, 2005) has a reprint of the 1992 article and demonstrates ways that other teachers in their Arizona group and around the country have applied their work. The goal of this way of learning from families has been, for nearly two decades, "to alter perceptions of working-class or poor communities and to view these households primarily in terms of their strengths and resources (or funds of knowledge)" (Gonzáles et al., 2005, p. x).

Teachers in the original funds of knowledge study group served working-class Mexican and Yaqui Indian families. The teachers and professors worked together as teams to learn about the home and community lives of the children and families by spending time there. They discussed how to create meaningful relationships with families by visiting homes, usually of three children each year, and entering into conversations, and not scripted interviews, with families. The conversations centered on three main areas of information, usually gathered in three visits:

1. Family history and work history (often through family stories about crossing the border, other moves, extended families, religious rituals and traditions, and informal as well as "hired" work experiences)
2. routine household activities (e.g., gardening, home and car repair, caring for children, and recreational activities)
3. Parents' views of their roles vis-à-vis their children (e.g., raising children, languages used at home, and schooling—both their own and their children's, in their home country as well as the United States if they were immigrants)

Teachers did their homework: They studied both the history of that border-region community and the labor histories of the families (especially related to mining and agriculture). The authors stressed that although they did gather information, the primary purpose of their home visits was "to foster a relationship of trust with the families" (Gonzáles et al., 2005, p. xi) throughout the year. As teacher–researchers, they also wrote about their home visits from their notes about what they observed in the neighborhood, the home, and their conversations. They taped these when the families gave permission—which they almost always did, once the teachers explained that they wanted to learn better ways to connect their child's home learning and school learning.

Writing is a great way to think through conversations with families. I can imagine writing things such as "how can I create opportunities in my classroom for Esperanza and other children, who assist their parents with selling pastries out of the home, to help them learn about money, making change, profit margins, and other mathematical skills?" or "Shawntina's grandma reminds me of how my brother learned to read from watching TV. Now that I know they love to watch their shows together, I'll show Shawntina how to check out the 'Reading Rainbow' videos from the library to watch with her grandma" or "I'm still thinking about Ran's comment about how different school is here from Beijing. I think I'll follow up with a phone call."

Teachers met in study groups throughout the year to discuss what they learned and to create thematic units of study based on the funds of knowledge they learned about in these home and community visits. One school found this process so valuable that it reorganized the school schedule so that each of the 40 teachers had one afternoon a month for household visits. Could your school do that?

So what were some of the funds of knowledge Moll et al. (1992) learned about and applied in designing curriculum and creating culturally relevant instructional support? Families had a wealth of knowledge about ranching, farming, mining, construction, and repair. Their business knowledge included appraising, renting and selling, labor laws, and building codes. Household management acumen included budgeting, child care, cooking, and repair. Many had knowledge of both contemporary and folk medicine —for people as well as animals. Religious knowledge included rituals, texts (especially the Bible), and moral and ethical understandings.

Classroom Funds of Knowledge Projects

Cathy Amanti (2005), a multiage intermediate-grades bilingual classroom teacher in Tucson, has been part of the Funds of Knowledge team from the beginning. In a chapter that details one curriculum unit she and her students developed, she emphasized that the focus grew out of family funds of knowledge for that year—another year, and certainly in another place, the unit might have little or no connection to students' lives.

That particular year, Cathy visited three homes and found a commonality that surprised her—horses. The Alfaro family owned three horses just a few blocks from the school. "Mr. Alfaro is teaching all his sons how to care for and ride horses. He himself is teaching his horse to dance. . . . The boys would like to be in a rodeo. . . . Mr. Alfaro participated in rodeos in Mexico" (p. 133). Another student, Fernando, rode and cared for horses each summer when he returned to stay with his grandparents on their ranch in Chihuahua. And at the Rivera home, Cathy was asked to wait until the family finished viewing a video a relative had taped of a horse race in Sonoyta, Mexico.

Based on this information, Cathy asked her class to write about their knowledge of horses and learned that many of her students knew a great deal and were very interested in horses. Together, they planned an integrated unit on horses. They built on their own extensive background knowledge, generated sophisticated questions, and conducted inquiry projects that addressed social studies (e.g., Spanish explorers and missionaries, history of saddles, local horse ordinances), language arts (e.g., online and library research, English/Spanish vocabulary, written and oral presentations), and science and math (e.g., horse anatomy, multicelled organisms, converting "hands" to inches and feet, and horse gestation and evolution). Families served as resources for their children, both on individual projects and in whole-class learning, including a live horseshoeing demonstration, a field trip to the home whose family owned three horses, and a viewing of the home video of the Mexican horse race. Students learned parents were valuable partners and relationships deepened—all from valuing family funds of knowledge.

In another Tucson classroom, kindergarten teacher Marla Hensley (2005) found a wealth of talent on home visits with Alicia, one of her African American students. Alicia's father, Jacob, was a groundskeeper and had helped the class plant a garden. During the home visits, Marla learned about his musical abilities: He played guitar and keyboard, and wrote poetry and songs. At Marla's invitation, Jacob and the kindergartners wrote a musical version of "The Little Red Hen" that combined gardening, music, and the study of breadmaking in various cultures. Another home visit revealed an African American foster parent skilled in dance; she choreographed the musical on her days off. From home visits, listening and talking with children, and even observing the clothes they wore, Marla enlisted family members as costume makers, stagehands, makeup experts, and breadmakers—including Navajo fry bread and tortillas. The students performed the musical five times, each time gaining more confidence in themselves and pride in their parents' contributions.

And now for the rest of the story. Alicia's father had not previously been "involved" in traditional school terms. He rarely went to PTA meetings, because he found the tone of the meeting negative. However, after his experience with Marla's class, Jacob wrote a musical about social issues for his fifth-grade son's class and decided to run for PTA president. He won. His more positive approach "inspired much greater attendance and a more balanced ethnic representation" (Hensley, 2005, p. 145). The PTA became more politically active, and Jacob was featured on the evening news. Because one teacher formed a relationship with him and valued his multiple talents, Jacob became a valued member of the school family and one of its most eloquent advocates.

Teachers in other parts of the country are learning about different family funds of knowledge. A group of 100 bilingual and nonbilingual teachers in New York City and Long Island visited homes of diverse families (Mercado, 2005), examining Puerto Rican households. A sample of the long list of family funds of knowledge included information about countries in Latin America, electrical wiring, music and dance (e.g., classical, jazz, salsa), computer technology, sales (e.g., Avon, Tupperware), needlework, teaching, translation and interpretation, diet and health, and community advocacy work.

In my consulting work with schools, I often ask educators to speculate on the funds of knowledge in the communities where they teach—and then learn from families. In a rural Georgia community, teachers identified both knowledge and interest in areas of agriculture, home child care, National Association of Stock Car Racing, World Wide Wrestling (WWW), and music (including rap, contemporary Christian, and country). With great insight and enthusiasm, this group of K–12 teachers, generated curricular questions and connections built on WWW: What are the physical skills needed, and how are they developed? How would you write a script for "SmackDown"? What are the economic issues related to wrestlers, management, merchandising, and fans? What is the connection among WWW champions, superheroes, and folk heroes in literature? One teacher learned that her students and their parents regularly watched wrestling together. She had a starting point.

On the Nelson Island village of Tooksook Bay, Alaska, educators identified different but equally salient family funds of knowledge among the Yup'ik Eskimo residents. These included small-engine repair (there are no cars on the tiny island); weather; weaving exquisite tundra grass baskets; carving whalebone sculpture; and essential skills for fishing, such as making and repairing hooks and nets and catching, curing, and cooking herring, king and silver salmon, and halibut. There are also issues that parents and teachers worry about, as there are everywhere: Is technology a blessing or a curse? What can we do to preserve our island's environment? Just as important as the content of family funds of knowledge and the issues they think are important is how children learn. Young Yup'iks learn primarily from observation and trial and error; verbal instruction is less important. This learning tradition has important ramifications for how teachers structure learning in school.

Projects in Kentucky and Houston

In this section we'll examine how teachers in other parts of the country have learned about family funds of knowledge. It may be helpful to consider four key findings from the work of Gonzáles et al. (2005) that are important as we think about forming relationships with families that support children's learning.

1. *All* families have important experiences, skills, and bodies of knowledge—"funds of knowledge." These funds are essential to the ways the families function in the home as well as in work and community settings. They are also resources for their children that the teacher can tap into.
2. Families use these funds of knowledge through social networks and relationships. Networks of family and friends were "flexible, adaptive, and active," and included multiple people outside the home. This told them that their students often had many "teachers" who knew them well in multiple contexts.
3. Teachers learn about how children learn. In most of the Mexican and Yaqui families, children were active participants and asked questions that guided their own learning (in contrast to Yup'ik children, who primarily observe, often silently, until they are ready to try the skill themselves, and to many European American middle-class children who learn primarily from verbal instruction).
4. *Confianza*—mutual trust—is essential in establishing a relationship between educators and family members. The home visits allowed teachers and parents/caregivers not only to learn about one another, but also to trust one another—that each adult was working in the child's best interest. Creating reciprocity (a healthy interdependency) is critical for the relationships to be enduring; in other words, although roles may not be the same, both teachers and parents give in ways that support one another and that support the child.

Appalachian Families in Kentucky. A group of teachers in rural Kentucky collaborated with Ellen McIntyre and Diane Kyle (McIntyre, Kyle, Moore, Sweazy, & Greer, 2001) at the University of Louisville to learn from Appalachian children and families. They visited some of the children's families in their homes—some as many as ten times a year—to learn their interests and how children learned at home, and incorporate what they learned into their teaching. They did not learn of monolithic "Appalachian Funds of Knowledge." What they learned were the unique ways each family operated: Which families helped with homework and which thought it was the school's job; social, emotional, and academic needs that might not be evident at school; and family knowledge such as farming procedures and the inner workings of the Veterans Administration.

This information influenced myriad teaching decisions, from what kind of homework went home with certain children (e.g., those who had help at home and those who worked independently) to a unit on Animals at Home to Agricultural Field Day involving community members. The learning was reciprocal. Family members asked teachers about many aspects of their children's schooling, and teachers were happy to provide information about school assignments, programs, and opportunities. McIntyre and her colleagues (2001) offered helpful points of discussion:

1. *Time.* There was no time provided during the school day, although some districts do build this into teaching schedules. Teachers visited families after school and on weekends. The teachers received stipends of $25 per visit from a grant. While there were more frequent visits early in each school year, the average number per teacher was two per month. This was adequate, teachers reported, because after the relationships were formed through home visits, "the parents are on our doorstep! . . . They all seem to pitch in. . . . The best thing, though, is that it's like we are all a family. The families know and trust us and each other" (p. 269).

2. *Learning about families.* Although much of what teachers learned helped them teach, they also learned some very troubling things as they became closer to families. Teachers need a support system to help them help families, such as a family resource coordinator or a school social worker, and they also need a support system to deal with their own emotions.

3. *What gets shared.* Family members grew to trust teachers who visited in their homes and formed relationships. This may place teachers in a moral dilemma. Teachers in Kentucky asked, "Should we use the information from home when reporting to special service teachers? Should we use the information to help families get help? Should we write only what parents tell us, or what we 'interpret' from what they are saying?" (p. 270). They decided to share only what benefited that child or family, but many dilemmas remained.

Houston Funds of Knowledge Project. A group of Houston teachers and teacher educators (Patterson, Baldwin, Gonzales, Guadarrama, & Keith, 1999) created the Houston Funds of Knowledge Project. Each teacher made at least three visits to the home of a student whose family had recently immigrated to the Houston area.

Elementary teacher Rubén Gonzales, who shared common cultural experiences with the Lopez family, focused on collaborative problem-solving. He began to talk with Rachel Lopez, Juan's mother, every morning during school breakfast. Rubén wrote, "Juan is an excellent student and is a leader in his own way. . . . Juan was having problems with his conduct in the classroom, so we were working together to solve the problem." Rubén wrote, "My theory and practice lie with a saying from the artist Amado Peña: '*Para los niños la semilla de nuestro futuro,*' or 'For the children, the seed of our future. . . .' Everything centers around [the] need to take care of our children. That is why the Funds of Knowledge project has been a dear part of my life. . . ." (Patterson et al., 1999, n.p.). Rubén become a principal and created a Funds of Knowledge Project as the primary professional development process in his school.

Liz Keith, a Houston middle-school English teacher, emphasized the importance of informal two-way conversations. "I have abandoned the accoutrement of the researcher in making home visits. . . . I have found that the tape recorder, notebook, and pen are barriers to communication. They seem to intimidate the families I have visited. They highlight the differences between us and create tension, which seems at odds with the purpose and goals of this kind of research." As her stance shifted, so did the relationship with her student's mother. "I never expected to find a friend in my research, but that's what happened" (Patterson et al., 1999, n.p.). This affected her relationship with her students:

> Somewhere along the way I began developing a more personal relationship with all my students. I think it's because I talk to them. We chat. They care to tell me when a grandmother dies or invite me to a *quinceañera*. They ask me what I did on the weekend, and I tell them. I am more responsive to my students in general. *What* I teach has not really changed so much as *how* I teach. My students have priority in my mind over my curriculum. (n.p., emphasis in original)

Building Respectful Relationships

The kind of relationships that the Rubén Gonzales and Liz Keith had with parents is so different from what I often experienced as a parent. Some of the teachers who wanted me to "be involved" in my children's discipline asked me to (1) sign a rather rigid and punitive schoolwide discipline contract (with which I didn't agree and didn't sign); (2) sign weekly behavior reports (which I did to keep some semblance of communication with the school, but knowing they made little difference to my child or to me), or (3) come in or talk on the phone (which I appreciated—we

Action Opportunity: Form Your Own Funds of Knowledge Study Team

1. From your perspectives as teachers and parents, generate what you know (or think you know) about the funds of knowledge of families in your school. It might be helpful to think in knowledge categories such as Scientific, Technology, Business, Education, Household Management, Communication, Medical/Health, Recreation, Music, and Religion to get started. Now, how can you learn the full extent of family funds of knowledge—things you would never have thought to put on your list? How can you establish mutual respect as you learn?

2. Learn from teams of experts like Gonzáles et al. (2005) how to learn from families. Role-play and debrief conversations ("Did that question seem intrusive—was I prying? What if they don't want to talk with me? I felt like an interviewer—how can I share more of myself?"). Parents and teachers, ask someone you feel comfortable with to have a "funds of knowledge" conversation with you.

3. After several informal chats, select one to three children in your classroom, school, or neighborhood. You might select the child whose family or cultural background you know the least about. Select families who are willing to talk with you. Arrange home visits; a chat over coffee in a neighborhood restaurant; or a trip to the park, where the children can play and adults can talk.

4. Write up each visit. It doesn't have to be a Pulitzer Prize winner. It could be a list of funds of knowledge, a story of the visit, questions, poems, ideas for teaching developed from funds of knowledge. Write in a form that is comfortable for you.

5. Make time at each of your study group or grade level or PTA meetings to read and discuss what you learned. How are you establishing trust? What funds of knowledge might you incorporate in the classroom? How does this young person learn at home, and how might that translate into classroom practices? Family members, how might you be involved in sharing your funds of knowledge?

6. Continue throughout the year. Repeat next year. The neighborhood changes; students change; families change. There will always be new funds of knowledge.

sometimes laughed, occasionally cried, and usually came up with a better plan to help the child we both were trying to support). It was through those conversations that I knew, "This teacher may be frustrated, but she really cares about my child."

What kind of relationship might you form, based on this concept of family funds of knowledge? Let's go back to your Jeremiah and his family, and your Ms. Gilcrest. We have some ideas now about how this tragic failure might have been prevented. Teachers, how might you go about learning from the families of students you have trouble reaching? Parents, how might you create a relationship with a teacher who does not reach out to you—how might you reach out? What difference might it make to our Jeremiahs?

These six steps are only one way to get started. What makes sense for you as an extended school family?

Developing Photography and Other Avenues to Learning with Families

This is my abuelito's secret place. . . . He lived with us a while ago. He found a secret place in the woods. It had seats. He read books there. We found him in his secret place. He said to come in.

(Allen et al., 2002, pp. 312–313)

Miguel's picture of an old car seat covered with pine straw in the woods behind his home is one of my favorites. We thought it was junk before he told us the story.

No one just looking at the picture could have guessed the story of this secret reading haven, nor the grandfather who transformed it and invited his grandchildren into the joys of a quiet place to read where "we hear grasshoppers and birds." We learned it only because Miguel's teacher provided him with a camera to capture his out-of-school life, because she asked him to tell her about the picture rather than interpreting it herself, and because she was part of the PhOLKS project.

In this chapter we continue to explore the concept of family funds of knowledge, "develop" photography as another avenue for learning, engage "cultural informants" to walk the avenue with us, and ponder the power of one teacher, one child, one family.

PHOTOGRAPHS OF LOCAL KNOWLEDGE SOURCES (PhOLKS)

A group of teachers in Athens, Georgia, formed a 2-year study group to investigate how we might use photography to learn family funds of knowledge. Vinette Fabregas, Karen Hankins, Gregory Hull, Linda Labbo, Hattie Lawson, Barbara Michalove, Steve Piazza, Cyndy Piha, Linda Sprague, Sybil Townsend, Carmen Urdanivia-English, and I (Allen et al., 2002) believed that the work of Moll, Gonzales, and their colleagues, which we discussed in the previous chapter, could help us connect students' out-of-school lives with their school lives.

The PhOLKS group served a diverse student population (in local terms, Black, Hispanic, White, and international students) primarily in low-income urban and rural schools. Our PhOLKS group itself was also diverse— women and men teaching prekindergarten to fifth grade, a media specialist, a teacher of English Language Learners, and two teacher educators, all with a range of life and teaching experiences. We were African American, Colombian, and European American; Christian and Jewish; originally from the Northeast, Midwest, and deep South; with childhoods from poor to privileged economically and educationally. This diversity was essential in mediating our understanding of cultural differences as we shared our students' pictures and the dictation or writing about the photos from the children and their family members.

With a small grant from the Spencer Foundation, we purchased three 35mm cameras, film, and film processing for each classroom. We invited children to take the cameras home and to photograph what was important to them in their homes and neighborhoods. Here are the steps, with variations, that we developed. Think about your students. How would you adapt such a project to learn about family funds of knowledge?

1. *Preparation.* We shared photographic essays with our students, such as *My Painted House, My Friendly Chicken, and Me* (Angelou, 1994) and *Daddy and Me: A Photo Story of Arthur Ashe and His Daughter* (Moutoussamy-Ashe, 1993). Some teachers read and discussed books that taught about photography, such as *Click!* (Gibbons, 1997); others invited parents who enjoyed photography to help children learn how to "see" through the camera's eye. First-grade classes read *I Am Six* (Morris, 1995), a big book about a first-grade class in New York City doing art, reading, music, and recess. Children then created their own version of *I Am Six* by photographing and writing about various activities in the classroom and on the playground; this provided the children with practice using the cameras at school. Some teachers brought in their own photographs and invited the children to share some of theirs. Carmen read from her memoir about growing up in Colombia. She also invited a reporter from a local Spanish-language newspaper, *Mexico Lindo*, to show her students ways to document their family and community histories.

2. *Photography and writing.* Three children took the cameras home every three days. Teachers had the film developed quickly and then asked children to write or dictate stories about their photos. They also invited parents or other family members to write about the pictures. Parents contributed detailed descriptions, memories, poetry, letters, and intimate personal stories. Steve Piazza, the media specialist, helped students scan their pictures using KidPics and create colorful presentations. Cyndy Piha expressed what many of us felt. "It was an incredibly moving experience for me to see my kids' lives. . . . It was like going from house to house. . . . I have a very wide range of children—economically, educationally, ethnically—and every single one of them has a very unique life, a very rich life outside of my classroom, and I forget that" (Allen et al., 2002, p. 315)

3. *Learning from photographs.* Our PhOLKS groups met monthly to learn from the children, their families, the photographs, and each other. We learned new ways for ourselves as teachers to connect with and reenvision children and family members. We documented how children explored personal, social, and cultural connections with each other, as when Najma taught his classmates about his Muslim religion through pictures of his mosque. We celebrated with children as they envisioned other possibilities for their lives, as when a seriously depressed fifth grader, Yessica, wrote about a picture of her family in Mexico: "Today my mother died. It's been 7 years . . . but I still remember it like it was yesterday. I am very sad." Her teacher, Carmen Urdanivia-English, encouraged her to write about how

---

Action Opportunity: Design a project that helps students teach you and each other about their out-of-school lives. How would you prepare students, together as parents and teachers? What technology would you use—regular, disposable, or digital cameras? Video cameras? Or if you don't have cameras, would you ask students to draw important scenes from their lives? Will students create photo essays, narratives, a poem to illuminate each picture, a verbal narration of a PowerPoint or iMovie presentation? What roles will you play as parents? As teachers? And most importantly—how will you learn together about family funds of knowledge, and how will that support student learning in new ways?

---

things would be different if her mother were there with her; Yessica began to envision some agency for herself and a new role for her absent mother.

However you design your "photographs of local knowledge sources" inquiry, I feel certain you will find, as we did, that what you learn has a direct impact on relationships among students, their families, and their teachers. And isn't that when teaching and learning are most powerful—when we have those relationships? Listen to some of those formed in the PhOLKS project.

Cyndy, a White teacher, worried about Kenesha, a Black child who often slept in class and lived in a trailer with no plumbing and too often no food. Other teachers at the school said her mother was never involved; they told Cyndy that the mother had been in special education when she attended the school. Cyndy's contact with the family was Kenesha's aunt, who also intimated that Kenesha's mother was not capable of raising her. Cyndy was delighted to discover that Mom, who had not previously communicated with her, wrote in her daughter's photo journal (Allen et al., 2002, pl. 317):

> My daughter name is Kenesha. . . . She stay with her mother that's me. . . . She is very sweet all the teacher and people love her because she is understanding and nice, polite, sweet, listen, smart. She have her good days & bad days but she is the sweetest child you like to spend time with. She go to church she sings in the choir at church members of the church love to hear her sing she sings so good you love her. She like to read and talk a lot. She loves dogs. She like to play with dolls. She love her new baby brother.

Cyndy did not ever meet Kenesha's mother, but after this letter, they began communicating frequently by notes and telephone. The mother wanted to know exactly how Kenesha was doing—"Keep letting me know," she told Cyndy. In turn, she said she would make sure Kenesha got more sleep. One photograph, one invitation to write, and one letter did not change Kenesha's life. The family still struggled, and so did Kenesha. But now there was a team—a teacher at school and Mom at home—who were working together to give Kenesha the best possible chance of learning.

Hattie Lawson also taught third grade. As an African American teacher, she felt she related very well to her Black students but worried that she didn't know the cultures of her Hispanic students. Through the PhOLKS project, she learned that the two communities shared many values, especially the importance of the extended family. She learned that adults in the Hispanic community often disciplined each other's children and that parents expected her to do the same.

Linda Sprague asked the parents of her kindergartners to photograph their children doing the household "jobs." Many students had a great deal of responsibility at home—much more than they did at school, and more than Linda, White and middle class, remembered her own children as having. The young mother of one struggling student, Demetrious, followed Linda's instructions quite conscientiously. This opened up a dialogue between Linda and Mom not only about this fund of knowledge —the expectation that even 5-year-olds have household responsibilities— but also about concerns they shared about Demetrious. Linda reflected, "I've learned that when parents ask, 'What can I do to help my child in school?' I need to have specific instructions and materials" (Allen et al., 2002, p. 318), as she had had in the photography project. Once this kind of communication was established, Demetrious made much greater progress, which Linda attributed to his mother working with him at home on the specific things she was teaching at school. She also began giving Demetrious (and his classmates) more responsibility for his own learning, the kind of responsibility he had developed at home.

VALUING FAMILY DIFFERENCES

Sometimes we don't know what we are "reading" without some help. We might not recognize the value of children translating for their parents or a car seat nestled in the woods. There is a great deal of research (see a review of studies by Boethel, 2003) that indicates parents from various cultural groups define their roles in educating their children differently from school definitions of "parental involvement." What educators might see as parents being uninvolved or uncaring—perhaps even abusive—might be viewed very differently by parents. How can we gain these cross-cultural insights?

At the risk of stating the obvious, one of the most important things we learn from sustained, respectful dialogue between educators and families is how unique each family is. Educators, if you were asked to describe the families of the children you teach, or parents, to describe the families who attend your child's school, what would you say? With that human urge to categorize (and judge), we might be tempted to say, "We only have six 'regular' families: the rest are single moms, kids living with grandparents, one boy who lives with his dad—and one gay family." These oversimplifications mask unique family structures. If we go back to the ways we thought and wrote about our own families, we probably valued—or at least identified as part of our story—what made our family unique. If someone was raised by her mother after her father died in Vietnam, did she describe her family solely as headed by a single mom? If someone's family received public assistance for several years, did he refer to his family solely as welfare recipients?

Casper and Schultz (1999), who conducted a 3-year study of the educational interactions of gay parents and their 3- to 7-year-old children's teachers, illustrated how limited single categories of families can be.

> A brother and sister being raised by two gay foster fathers in rural Oklahoma have a discrete experience being part of a gay-headed family; it is certainly different, in so many ways, from that of the son of an urban single lesbian mother who chose to become pregnant with the help of an unknown sperm donor. Adults who were married and raised children to various points of development before coming out bring yet other experiences and frames of reference to their children's blended family experience. (p. 6)

Similarly, we might think of parents who are divorced as being alike. Yet if we think of the people we know, we recognize that each divorced family is different: some are bitter, some amicable, some remarried one or more times. Now consider further complicating factors such as religious beliefs and practices concerning divorce, cultural practices related to extended and blended families, and issues unique to adoptive parents. "The complications that can arise over parental conflicts about biological and nonbiological ties can be extremely threatening to young children," noted Casper and Schultz (1999, p. 6). They pointed out that as damaging as custody battles may be in heterosexual families, those headed by gay and lesbian partners who are separating in most states do not even have the courts to protect parental or child rights.

Nobody who has been teaching more than a week would still be likely to define a family as a mother, father, and one or more children. Our society includes a rich proliferation of possibilities: a dad and daughter, six siblings with two moms and two dads in a blended family where the children split their time between two residences, an aunt and grandma raising several younger family members. Educators and families in a school who get to know each other in these more complex ways—not as families in general, but the very families in this particular learning community—have a stronger foundation for supporting the child as a learner.

Once we get to know each other, how do we use information about families in order to teach children? What assumptions do we make, consciously or unconsciously? When a first grader "borrows" a GI Joe action figure from another child's desk, do we draw different conclusions if the child is in a two-parent home than we would if he is being raised by his grandmother because his dad is in prison? Would we look at a fifth-grade boy who plays jump rope with the girls at recess differently if he is being raised by two moms rather than by a mom and dad? Remember Karen Hankins's two students, Eric and Tommy (see Chapter 2), and her different expectations for them as struggling readers, based on what she knew of the families? Sometimes we need more information, a different perspective, than home visits or frequent phone conversations can supply.

LEARNING FROM OTHER CULTURAL INFORMANTS

Families and children are educators' first and most important teachers about home cultural norms and values, but sometimes they are not sufficient. Often there are other cultural informants in our communities, schools, or right there in the classroom. Teaching assistants, teachers, secretarial and custodial staff, parent volunteers, and other people in the school who have different cultural experiences from our own can become valuable teachers as we seek to increase our "cultural intelligence." Especially if we are new to a community as a teacher or parent, we can seek out people who are willing to talk with us about cultural norms and practices that can help us create the partnerships we value. We might ask questions like, "Where I grew up teachers didn't want parents teaching their kids to read, because they said it would confuse them. What about at this school—what do teachers expect?" or "I am noticing that many parents here seem stricter with their children than where I came from. How do parents discipline their children in this community? What do you think they expect from me as their children's teacher?"

Cristina Igoa, an ESL teacher, learned about cultural practices not only from families themselves but also from other cultural informants. One area of learning was that cultural norms for discipline varied widely. Maybe you've seen the same thing in your community—some teachers and parents value cautionary tales or scolding, some put children in "time out," some employ physical punishment. These different philosophies and practices can create a great deal of tension for all concerned—especially the child. Igoa (1995) gave the example of students from Samoa. Many of those she taught had difficult home situations and were defiant in school. Teachers wanted to enlist the help of parents but were reluctant to call home for fear that the children would receive severe punishment; one parent had previously cut off an inch of a girl's hair after a call from Igoa that she had been rebellious, and another had kicked his son out of the house "because he had shamed the family by his actions at school" (p. 59).

The teachers were torn between protecting their students from harsh punishment and wanting to work with families to help children get along with their peers—and their teachers. Igoa reported, "Gradually, and with great care, I began to speak to the Samoan parents in such a way that they knew I had the child's best interests in mind" (p. 59). She also began doing her homework to learn more about Samoan culture. She talked with a cultural anthropologist at the local university and learned that throwing a child out of the house had a different purpose and meaning in Samoan culture than in the United States. The child usually went to the home of someone in the extended family for a "cooling-off" period. Igoa saw this "punishment" in a new light—like removing a disruptive child from the classroom. I suspect that there are other cultures where this kind of cooling-off period is a common way of defusing volatile situations. A friend of one of our sons lived with us for several months under similar circumstances.

Igoa continued her research. She learned that the Samoan church was the center of family life for many of her students and that the pastor could be a valuable ally—especially for her male Samoan students, who "from age 10 onward begin the cultural process of not bending to the authority of women" (p. 60). Consequently, she enlisted the fathers of some of her students as mediators of their school behaviors. She watched films of life in Samoa and made accommodations in the classroom that gave students more physical space and engaged them in storytelling and making filmstrips about their native country. As she explained the effects of her learning on developing culturally relevant teaching, Igoa showed how one young man, F'aatui, went from a silent, sullen, and disruptive student who went home for lunch and rarely returned, to one who became so engrossed in recording his story that he became "the elder storyteller of his class" (p. 63). F'aatui's adjustment to school (and the school's adjustment to F'aatui) came about because of his father, minister, teacher, and other cultural informants Igoa consulted.

Action Opportunity: The most important part for me in the commonly used KWHL process—What do we *know*, *what* do we want to learn, *how* can we find out, what have we *learned*—is the *how*. So take a little time now to brainstorm—*how* can we learn aspects of culture in our school and community that could make a difference for students? Who are possible cultural informants in the school and community? How else can we learn together—what can we read, with whom can we talk, what media (movies, TV shows, etc.) might lead us to deeper understanding of each other?

SOLO SNAPSHOTS: LEARNING ONE CHILD, ONE FAMILY, ONE TEACHER AT A TIME

It is wonderful to be involved with a project like the various funds of knowledge teacher collaborations we've been discussing. If you are reading about this with a group of teachers and/or parents, you have just that opportunity—to create your own funds of knowledge process, to get together to discuss what you are learning, to plan curriculum based on funds of knowledge for your whole grade level, whole disciplinary area, or even your whole school. But many outstanding teachers all over the United States—perhaps all over the world—learn from families without being part of such a support group. In this section, we'll meet some of them and see what a difference one teacher, connecting with one family, on behalf of one child, can make.

Antonio

Paula Murphy was a Chapter 1 reading teacher in an alternative junior high school in New York City when she met 13-year-old Antonio. He stopped her in the hall, ascertained that she was a reading teacher, and then requested, "I need help in reading. Can I go to your class?" (1994, p. 75). Murphy learned that Antonio had a broad vocabulary and information base, had clearly articulated thoughts, and was fluent in oral Spanish and English, yet he struggled as both a reader and a writer. As she got to know him better, she learned that he had been homeless for the past 5 years, had missed a great deal of school, and had been moved in and out of bilingual programs. His teachers now thought he should be placed in special education. When his family moved, the school system made little effort to keep him in his current school—until his teacher intervened.

Murphy decided that to teach Antonio, she had to learn about his life. She began making home visits at different locations as the family moved from a shelter to a friend's apartment to other temporary housing. She learned that Antonio's mother and his stepdad often helped him and a sibling with homework and that his mother wrote short stories (which she asked Murphy to help her publish). In spite of extreme financial in-stability, Antonio's family provided him with emotional support and edu-cational encouragement. Murphy designed a reading program for Antonio that actively involved his parents and stayed in close communication with them. "After one year—and despite the constant moving and absences—Antonio's reading and writing skills improved significantly," Murphy re-ported (p. 82). She mused:

> As a Puerto Rican raised and educated in Puerto Rico, I felt that sharing the culture and the language of my Latino students was enough to understand their world. . . . I learned . . . there are many things foreign to me about the children I teach. I know nothing about growing up poor, homeless and in an environment of violence. . . . I learned of my responsibility to understand, not only my students' ethnic culture, but their community culture as well. . . . Children like Antonio will continue to be poor because the education they need to succeed is being denied by the same system established to educate them. (p. 87)

What can we learn from studying one child? Connecting with one fam-ily? Who are our Antonios, our students whose home cultures may be be-yond our experience unless we reach out?

Miguel

Like Antonio, 11-year-old Miguel was bilingual. He lived with his parents and two younger siblings in Chicago. As the strongest English speaker and reader in the family since their move to the United States, Miguel often interpreted letters and other documents for his parents. For example, Miguel helped his mother read the letter from school asking par-ents to cooperate in getting students to observe the dress code. Using a combination of Spanish, English, and gestures, he explained that girls may not wear midriff blouses or spaghetti strap shirts, that sleeveless blouses must begin at "the junction between the arm and the shoulder," and that "students not in compliance will be asked to comply" (Orellana, Reynolds, Dorner, & Meza, 2003, pp. 26–27). Miguel and his mother worked through the letter with its unfriendly, authoritative language ["further steps will be taken by the administration to get the student in compliance" (p. 27)], jointly constructing meaning.

Given the barrage of paper that schools send home on a daily basis (testing reports, student work, newsletters, assignments, permission forms, and policy statements like this one), one wonders how often Miguel and students like him serve as translators. According to Orellana and colleagues (2003), who studied 18 students over several years, this is an almost daily occurrence for children in immigrant families. Contrast this with most English-only families, where students have the (often neglected) responsibility of simply getting the papers home, and parents have the luxury of glancing through the papers to see what needs a response, what goes on the refrigerator, and what goes in the trash. Interactions like this, and countless others the authors documented, support the claim that many Latino families in the United States value education highly and support their children in the ways they think are most appropriate. For further examples, you might read work by Concha Delgado-Gaitan such as *Literacy for Empowerment: The Role of Parents in Children's Education* (1990) and *School Matters in the Mexican American Home* (1992).

How could knowing more about our bilingual students' literacy interactions with family members lead to better home–school connections? First, Orellana and colleagues (2003) suggested that teachers can bring these skills to the classroom by encouraging students to work in small groups to "interpret" and paraphrase written instructions in textbooks—a common and difficult school task that would likely benefit English-only speakers as well. Second, students could go over important notes such as the dress-code policy statement in class, using it as a reading text of a particular genre—the "official institutional language" genre that all of us deal with all our lives—to analyze, paraphrase, and interpret. This practice would assist all children in interpreting for parents what the notes from school mean and what parents need to do to follow up. A third possibility that builds the home–school connection might be asking students to bring print items from home to collaboratively read, paraphrase, and interpret. They might bring letters from family living outside the United States or materials from religious, social, or civic groups in which families participate. Encourage students to read and discuss these materials with family members before bringing them to school.

Keith

Another example of one teacher and one family working together on a child's behalf is the collaboration Jane Rogers developed with Keith (pseudonym) and his family. Keith, a child with autism, entered Jane's special-education resource room at age 7 literally kicking and biting, speaking only two words, having been tethered in his previous class because of his tendency to run away. His IEP that first year listed only objectives related to behavior, but Rogers offered him full membership in the literate community she created in her classroom through songs, chants, children's literature, and daily writing. She invited Keith's parents to be equal partners in his education, which they did for all of the 3 years he was in her class. (Rogers, 2000) wrote:

> As concerned parents, they wanted to assist in Keith's education. They attended formal meetings weekly about Keith's adjustment and needs for the first year. . . . Keith's mother met informally with me every morning as she brought Keith into the school. She shared problems, concerns and successes that Keith had at home. . . . We often talked about how his evenings went at home and how I should adapt my day accordingly. . . . We also talked about the books that Keith took home with him from the library. His mother shared with me his response to the books that she read to him. . . . They also collected data . . . and collaborated with me on the many drafts of this study. (p. 57)

One of the unique and highly successful invitations to literacy began with the suggestion from Keith's parents that Jane incorporate the "AZ video method" of teaching children with autism by taping an object–word association and playing it repeatedly, capitalizing on the need children with autism have for high repetition. Jane modified the AZ method. She videotaped every child in the room reading with Keith, a daily "reading buddy" activity. Keith took each book and video home and watched them multiple times with various members of his family. His parents kept a log of interactions during the viewings, words he said during or after the viewing, and so on. Keith made remarkable progress, not only in language (55 words and signs) and emergent reading and writing but also in interacting with his peers during "buddy reading." School and home support complemented each other to such a degree that Keith's sister Katie, noting his increasing vocalization, spent a weekend teaching him to say his alphabet!

Do you remember Karen Hankins, whom we met in the Chapter 1? She often visits the homes of her students. On one such visit, she talked with

---

Action Opportunity: As a school community (parents, staff, administrators, students), plan how teachers could make home visits a cornerstone of communication at your school. What are the benefits? What are the barriers? What would it take—today—to make that commitment?

Randel and his mother. They live in a housing area people tended to talk about with lowered voices: "He lives over there in—*Oakdale.*" As Hankins explained Randel's very positive report card, he pointed to the walls, where there were alternating pictures of Jesus and the Reverend Martin Luther King Jr., and asked his mother,

> "Am I like him, mama, am I growing up good?" She hugged him to her, saying, "Yes, baby, you are. Mama's so proud. You are a fine and wonderful son. You just keep on learning your books and acting right. You'll go somewhere." (Hankins, 2003, p. 41).

Hankins wrote, "I don't know if he meant growing up like Jesus or like MLK, but clearly the social, political, and spiritual are not separate entities in this household" (p. 41). Visits like this are important to Hankins. They give her a glimpse of her students through the eyes of parents and their high expectations. They also provide avenues for connecting with the child at school. Indeed, this visit was pivotal to Hankins's understanding of Randel's remarkable role in her classroom that year. He became "The Preacher." This visit—one teacher, one mother, one child—made a difference.

CHAPTER 5

Engaging in Genuine Dialogue

Humanity lies in the
Restless,
Impatient,
Continuing,
Hopeful
Inquiry
[We] pursue
In the world,
With the world,
And with each other.

I created this "found poem" from the writings of Paulo Freire (1970, p. 58) because he gives me hope. Some days I need it.

One such day was the day I attended my youngest son's middle school open house. In each class—five different rooms—the teacher read the same rules and consequences. Period. No discussion. In each classroom, printed versions of the rules were the only "decoration" on the wall, except in the language arts classroom, which had a poster of long and short vowel sounds —this was middle school, mind you. By the fifth period, I was ready to scream, enroll my child in another school, plead for an audience with the principal—"Yes, now, at 9:22 at night!" I did none of those things. I went home and cried for my son.

In this chapter and the next, you are going to meet some teachers who make connecting with parents a high priority, teachers who have developed very effective ways of establishing meaningful relationships with family members, teachers who nonetheless sometimes failed, as we all have. I met these teachers through an excellent book by Sara Lawrence-Lightfoot, *The Essential Conversation: What Parents and Teachers Can Learn from Each Other*. Lawrence-Lightfoot (2003) interviewed parents, observed parent–teacher conferences, and studied ten teachers regarded by colleagues and parents as "skilled, empathic, and caring" teachers who "reached out to and communicated with families, developed strategies and practices that honored parental knowledge and wisdom; and turned the largely symbolic parent-teacher conversations into meaningful, expressive exchanges" (p. xxvi). I learned a lot from those teachers. I think you will, too.

CREATING AND SUSTAINING DIALOGUE

One of those teachers, Sophie Wilder, told of a very different open house from the one I described, one where she worked hard at communicating, but still one where both the parent and Sophie probably went home and cried. Teaching fifth- and sixth-grade students for the first time, Sophie had "one of those classes." The students had a reputation as a "tough group . . . unruly, angry, and mean and disrespectful to one another" (Lawrence-Lightfoot, 2003, p. 47). She had worked from the beginning of school to teach respect, kindness, and a sense of community. Well aware through years of previous experience of the importance of clear communication with parents, Sophie carefully and thoroughly detailed her focus to parents at the fall open house, explaining the relationship between the atmosphere in the classroom and academic excellence. Before she could finish, a mother said contemptuously, "Did it ever occur to you that if you believed in our children and really thought that they could do these things, that they would quite naturally do them? Why do you think that you need to continue to preach to them?" (p. 48).

What would you have done at this point as the teacher, or as another parent in the room, or as the frustrated parent who cried out?

Recognizing Oppression

One of the most renowned teachers in the world, Brazilian educator Paulo Freire (1970), challenged me more than anyone I know to think about my interactions with others and to create genuine dialogue rather than my natural tendency to debate (and try to win). Freire wrote that our "vocation is to be more fully human" (p. 41). We may be hairdressers, full-time parents, professors, sanitation or aeronautical engineers; we may work for the IRS or the DOE or the local pub; but our *vocation* is to be more fully human. That means to me that I have to make a conscious effort in every interaction. Freire worked with powerful politicians, peasants who were learning to read and write, and teachers all over the world. He looked at the structures in society in terms of people who were oppressed and people who oppressed others (and sometimes one person can be both, depending on the circumstances). He learned some of the pitfalls in the struggle to "humanize" society.

1. As Freire noted, people who have been oppressed themselves often become oppressors because they only see two kinds of people —those with power and those without. When we gain power as parents, as teachers, as administrators, we too often see "other" people as threatening, incompetent, or lazy. Sometimes when I think about why a teacher treats his students in ways I know he would not want to be treated, I wonder if teachers perhaps treated him the same way. If I berate you for being lazy, am I echoing a painful evaluation of my own work ethic by my seventh-grade teacher? Likewise, does a parent who experienced failure in school assert her authority over a teacher by demanding certain concessions for her child?
2. There is a related tendency for the new group in power to become dominating and bureaucratic. What, you say—schools a bureaucratic organization? Let's dig a little deeper for this point. If you are a teacher, even an "experienced" (i.e., old like me) teacher, you are part of the new regime. You are part of what is an increasingly demonized and oppressed class, with teachers being regulated and blamed as never before. This may also be true if you are part of a parent group with power—you may not be speaking for all parents, especially those who are not as visible at school and "involved" as you are. It's easy to see how, in an effort to assert autonomy and command respect, we may become part of a dominating—rather

than dialoguing—bureaucracy. Our very vows to "do things differently" than they were done to us may evolve into a new and oppressive "right way."

3. As teachers, we may see ourselves as "emancipators" who work *for* rather than *with* oppressed people—poor families, struggling students, marginalized cultural groups. We work hard for our students and their parents because we "know" what they need to be successful. The problem is, unless we work together, no one is going to be successful. So how do we avoid this pitfall? Freire (1970) stressed that those not of the oppressed group can work in solidarity with the oppressed only if they enter into the situation and really come to know the people—only if they "risk an act of love" (p. 35).

I know so many teachers who risk that act of love. They love, or learn to love, students others cannot love and parents who do not love them but see them as the enemy, like the mother who confronted Karen Hankins in the first chapter. How do they do it? Primarily though dialogue.

Dialogue, according to Freire, is very different from a conversation. In genuine dialogue, people come to understand another person's perspective. They may even change their own perspective. Freire's definition of dialogue is the encounter between people, mediated by the world in which they live (in our cases, the multiple worlds of classroom, school and district, home, and workplace), "in order to name the world" (p. 76). This naming is important—it is saying "there is an elephant in the room" or "the emperor has no clothes." We have to name structures that harm our children and confront acts of oppression perpetrated by social and educational systems.

Oppression seems like a very harsh word, maybe overly dramatic, certainly very political. Are we really part of a system that oppresses children and families? Let's Google it (and question ourselves). Definitions of *oppression* on the Web:

> Oppression is the arbitrary and cruel exercise of power. While the term is usually used to describe wrongful acts of government, oppression is rarely limited solely to government action. Oppression is most commonly felt and expressed by a widespread, if unconscious, assumption that a certain class of people are inferior. (en .wikipedia.org/wiki/Oppression) *In one of my graduate classes, a teacher in a county where fewer than half the students graduated from high school justified ability tracking in her school after reading of its deleterious effects because "somebody has to collect the garbage and dig the ditches and it's probably going to be those kids."*

An unjust and systematic excessive exercise of power against an identified group of people, such as Jews, homosexuals, or disabled people, where the laws, attitudes towards and treatment (including portrayal) of this group all reinforce this discriminatory situation. (www.bfi.org.uk/education/resources/teaching/disability/further/disabilityglossary.php) *Have you ever thought, "You know, sometimes when I'm in the teachers' lounge, I cringe at the way we talk about children who read so far below grade level. It is like they are the villains that are making us all look bad with their low test scores. And the things we say about their parents . . ."*

The absence of choices, the experience of being systematically limited and restricted by intentional, external forces. (www.letswrap.com/LetsWRAP/Spring97/isms.htm) *I worry that sometimes when we lay out the "choices" to parents about their children, there really aren't any: "He can repeat first grade or fall farther and farther behind" or "We hope you will sign these papers for the behavioral testing battery; otherwise, poor Jenny seems destined for hours each day in the "Opportunity Room."*

Sometimes as parents our advocacy can become oppression. We have inside knowledge; we know the principal or an influential teacher. This is not an abstract point for me. I have worked with my local school district for 20 years. On occasion I asked for "privileges" for my children by requesting a particular teacher. When I asked for my child to have a great teacher, I used the power of my position in society to keep someone else from having that teacher. This created "an absence of choices" for another child who was "limited and restricted by intentional, external forces." I was that external force. We have to name acts of oppression, whether it is school rules, district mandates, federal guidelines, or our own practices that oppress. Until we name something, we really can't have a dialogue, and without a dialogue, we can't change anything.

Risking Dialogue

Genuine dialogue is not easily achieved; people more often debate, talk past each other, or otherwise fail to meet Freire's (1970) conditions of true dialogue:

Love   Freire is talking about "a profound love for the world" and for people (p. 77). This is the kind of love that leads many of us into teaching—and the love that fades to cold ashes when we burn out.

Humility   This one is so hard for me! Is it for you? Don't you really believe, whether you are entering into the conversation as a teacher or as a parent, that you really understand the situation and know the solution better than the other person? Yet Freire challenged me: "How can I dialogue if I always project ignorance onto others and never perceive my own?" How can I hear in a way that allows me to change my thinking, to consider other perspectives "if I am closed to—and even offended by—the contribution of others?" (pp. 78–79)

Faith   Freire called for "an intense faith in [humankind]," a faith going into a relationship, whereas "*trust* is established by dialogue" throughout the relationship (pp. 79–80). Teacher Sophie Wilder (Lawrence-Lightfoot, 2003) had faith that parents knew their children better than she did, that "every bit of information that I get from parents is always helpful in filling in the spaces of what I can't see and don't know" (p. 69). I love the analogy Sophie uses for the kind of relationship she wants to create with parents. She said that when parents and teachers establish trust through dialogue, it is like "close neighbors chatting over the back fence"—casual, natural, a "loose kind of love" (p. 71).

Hope   Hope is an active condition, an expectation that through dialogue the world will become better; hopelessness is silence that can indicate dehumanizing despair. If I go into a conference without believing that the teacher will understand, or that the parent will work with the child, or that the child really has the capacity to learn, then there will be no hope, no dialogue.

Critical Thinking and Action   There is no more crucial time to be able to think critically than when the two most important sets of people in a child's life, parents and teachers, are talking together about decisions that will have profound implications for that child's life.

Okay, we've got to get back to Sophie now, prepared with this way of looking at dialogue that gives us hope.

What about Sophie, what did she do? Although she felt "hurt and speechless," she answered the mother softly, "I do care about these kids, and I'm sorry if I'm not getting that across." Later that evening, she tried talking individually with the angry mom: "Wow, it sounds as if you're feeling pretty upset about this stuff." When that elicited no response, she continued, "It sounds as if I have to do a better job appreciating your son." The mother eventually talked about her frustration. "By the end of the evening, she left feeling as if she had gotten something off of her chest," Sophie recalled. "But I ended up feeling raw and raging" (p. 48).

Maybe this kind of scene is why school-sponsored interactions with parents such as open houses and conferences have too often come to be ritu-

Action Opportunity: Role-play Sophie and Mom's encounter. Two people start in the center of the room, with others in a circle around them. Role-play the scene as written at the beginning of this section. Now, at any point, someone from the circle can tap either Sophie or Mom on the shoulder and take her place. The new person should come to the center with a way of moving genuine dialogue forward. It may be naming some oppressive practice, expressing faith in the other person (or the kids), or thinking critically together of new ways of looking at the situation. It may mean an act of humility. Your goal is to work toward dialogue. There is no one answer.

alized events with little genuine dialogue. Maybe that's why my son's middle school teachers only read the rules. Dialogue is one of the most difficult things in the world to achieve. Yet it is central to our very humanity.

CREATING OPPORTUNITIES FOR DIALOGUE

What are ways teachers and parents create opportunities for genuine dialogue? Why do some schools actually forbid the "hand-off" of students from parents to teachers each morning when this could be a place for regular dialogue? It is, of course, limited; many students ride the bus, and middle and high school students might feign death rather than being seen walking in the hall with their parents. But if it's possible, create the space and see what happens to communication.

Encouraging Hand-Off Chats

Concha Delgado-Gaitan (2004), who fosters and studies effective home–school partnerships, noted, "In communities where children walk to school, many Latino parents make it a point to walk with them. They take that opportunity to talk with the teacher and check in about their child's progress" (p. 28) They may ask for clarification about an assignment, share something that is going on in the family ("We had a birthday party for her grandmother last night, so she might be a little sleepy today"), make a connection to the curriculum ("He is very excited about the unit on machines and wondered if you would like his uncle to show the kids how a backhoe works"), or discuss a behavioral issue ("We talked with her about how it distracts the other students when she sings loudly during silent reading time; she will save her singing for music class and the playground"). Hand-off times when the parent transfers the child to the care of the teacher (e.g., when he or she walks the child to the classroom or when the teachers transfers the child back to the parent at the end of the day) can also be a prime time for teachers to share a positive learning example ("Yesterday the whole decimal system just clicked—she was going around the room translating everything into decimals!") or suggestions for working together at home ("We're studying chemical compounds in everyday living; as he is reading the book, you might ask him explain it using household examples").

Issuing Frequent Invitations

Many teachers work hard at creating regular opportunities for dialogue. Lawrence-Lightfoot (2003) described Jane Cross's approach. Jane invited parents to come in any morning they could from 8:00 to 8:30 during "choice time." Parents could read with their child, do a project in the art corner, or talk with Jane about something that concerned them. Teachers who invite parents into the classroom or encourage conversation during the hand-off learn so much. Maybe Juanita had been having trouble sleeping and was a little cranky, or maybe Don had a letter from his aunt in Bosnia that he wanted to share with the class.

Molly Rose, a first-grade teacher first in a suburban and then in an urban school, created multiple opportunities to dialogue with parents (Lawrence-Lightfoot, 2003). Molly expected every parent to be involved, and they were, I think because the invitations were plentiful, varied, and genuine. "Almost everything I do with parents is with the child at the center," Molly explained (p. 61). These are her invitations to dialogue:

> *Letter to the child before school starts*, telling what Molly did during the
> summer; for example, "I read a lot of good books, I went swimming, and I went hiking" (p. 62). She drew a picture of herself hiking and asked the children to draw pictures of themselves and have an adult help them write back to her. When parents and their children came to school, they found these letters decorating the classroom.
> *Getting-to-know-you conferences* with each parent or guardian during the
> first month. "I try very hard not to talk at all. This is purely a listening conference. . . . The parents are the experts, and I'm seeking their wisdom and their guidance. . . . I'm saying come and tell me all about your child," Molly said (p. 62). She asked for, and got, 100% participation because, as she explained, "I make myself avail-

able any time of the day, from early morning to late at night. We
work through all kinds of scheduling complications. . . . When they
break an appointment or do not show, I have no problem with that.
I don't take it personally. We work until we can find another time"
(p. 63).

Weekly communications. Each Monday, children took home an envelope
of their work from the previous week. The envelope had a note
from Molly about the child as a learner on one side and space for
parents to write a response on the other side. While parental responses were "uneven," Molly felt that it was important for her to
observe each child carefully enough to write about his or her development. In addition, Molly often called home to report "wonderful news," like to read a new piece of the child's writing or to
invite a parent to the classroom to see how well his daughter was
reading.

Each Friday, Molly sent home a one-page Rose Room Letter
with some of the usual information parents need to know about
field trips and so on. But most of the space was reserved for what
Molly thought was most important to good communication among
parents, children, and herself: "Ask Me . . ." Molly created this
unique feature, which includes 10 to 12 questions parents can ask
their children about what went on in their school lives that week.
When the students visited the arboretum, "Ask Me . . ." included
questions such as "How were the trees at the arboretum different
from when you observed them in the fall? Why are the trees changing: How do you think they will be different when you observe
them in the spring?" Just think how different this is from what we
usually ask: "How was your field trip?" Answer: "Fun. Jesse ate
five doughnuts and got sick on the bus."

Student-led conferences. Read about this in the next chapter!

Action Opportunity: In small groups, dream a little. Teachers, write Every
Teacher's Dream of Parental Involvement. Parents, write Every Parent's
Dream of Involvement in My Child's Education. Together, brainstorm Every
Child's Dream of Parents and Teachers Working Together. What features
are the same? Different? Possible? Which features would have the most
impact on student learning?

DAMAGING OR DESTROYING DIALOGUE

When my daughter was in third grade, her teacher began her conference with me with a long list of problems—more what I would call gripes.
Rachel talked too much. She didn't always comply quickly. She complained
about "boring" assignments. Finally, I asked, with thinly veiled sarcasm,
"Is there anything she does well?" "She is an excellent student!" her teacher
replied quickly—and with a look that conveyed, "But you already know
that. You are here so I can tell you all the problems." Trying to find constructive ground, and being pretty sure I wasn't going to get my daughter
to stop talking (she's now a public relations director), I asked when they
were going to start writing. "Rachel really loves to write stories," I said.
Somewhat taken aback by my ignorance, the teacher explained, "Oh, they
are learning to write sentences this year. They don't write paragraphs until
next year."

We had both "explained" some things about Rachel and played our
roles as parent and teacher, but there had been no dialogue, no understanding, no neighborly conversation over the back fence. I didn't feel like she
knew, much less liked, my daughter. She did not think I was a very good
parent.

Communicating the Wrong Thing

As hard as we work at establishing two-way communication, we sometimes fail. I usually have very good rapport with students in my university classes; I work hard at it. One semester, midway through, I noticed
that one young woman, Becky, had become quietly hostile toward me. I
couldn't figure out what had caused the change in our relationship. When
I asked students to write to me midterm about how the course (and I) was
or wasn't meeting their needs, I was shocked to learn about what had created the breach between Becky and me. She referred to a time when the
class had been working intently in groups and it was time to come together
as a whole group. I whistled, the standard high–low whistle intended to
gain my students' attention. Becky wrote, "I couldn't believe you *whistled*
at us. People whistle at dogs. I am not a dog." I have never used that signal
again.

An experienced second-grade teacher in a working-class school, Jennifer Austin had a reputation for building strong relationships with parents. She celebrated students' individual strengths when she talked with
parents, and she was also honest about their challenges. Parents appreciate both. During one conference, however, an unfortunate word destroyed
the potential dialogue. Jennifer was talking with a mother about her son

and said that he was "needy." Lawrence-Lightfoot (2003) noted an immediate shift in the conversation. "Jamie's mom's body stiffens and her jaw gets tight. She tried to keep her voice even. 'He gets pretty much attention at home. We always have our private time'" (p. 57). One word. Dialogue was destroyed by using a label instead of describing actions; for example, "Yesterday he stayed by my side during recess, asking for reassurance about the math lesson; I told him he was figuring it out just fine, but he must need something more from me. Do you have any insights?"

Communicating Across Social Class

The need for better dialogue was evident in several of the school–home interactions Annette Lareau (2003) documented in her study of how social class affected family lives. In general, she learned that middle-class parents advocated forcefully for their children. They regularly requested or demanded particular teachers, different teaching or grading methods, less or more homework. They paid for private testing to get their children into special classes and private tutoring to help them succeed. For example, Ms. Marshall, an African American computer analyst, talked with all of her daughter Stacy's teachers to let them know that Stacy had a slow, methodical learning style and that she would need additional time on tests. Lareau concluded, "Middle class mothers were often very interventionist" (p. 163). Their interventions, however, were not always welcomed or heeded by the school.

Melanie Handlon, a fourth grader from a middle-class European American family, struggled in school. Her mother spent 2 to 3 hours every night doing homework with her. She requested spelling lists from the teacher 5 weeks in advance, so Melanie could study them. She closely monitored her daughter's schooling and intervened often on her behalf. However, one of Melanie's teachers, Ms. Nettles, saw Melanie's mom not as a model of involvement but as a big part of Melanie's problem. While Ms. Nettles cheerfully cooperated with every request, she was dismayed that Melanie was late for school most days, that she was absent for 30 days with an illness the teachers questioned, and that her mom had not returned the paperwork necessary to have Melanie tested for a learning disability. Ms. Handlon thought Ms. Nettles was destroying her daughter's self-confidence, giving an unreasonable amount of homework, and failing to explain concepts adequately. Ms. Nettles thought Melanie's mother was overprotective and noncompliant; she said, "I think a lot of Melanie's problem is her mother" (Lareau, 2003, p. 195). She did not know how much time Ms. Handlon spent working with Melanie at home. In short, there was no dialogue—no understanding of each other's perspective, no collaborative problems solving—just the parent telling the teacher what she needed to do and the teacher telling the parent what she needed to do. I wonder if anyone asked Stacey for her thoughts?

In contrast, poor and working-class parents in Lareau's study rarely gave advice or made specific demands of teachers. Some were afraid they would do the wrong thing for their children, some placed great faith in teachers as professionals, and some feared retribution from the school or other government agencies. However, this deference did not lead to dialogue. Lareau (2003) noted, "Mothers who nod in silent agreement during a parent-teacher conference may at home, and within earshot of their children, denounce the educator as unfair, untrustworthy, or mean" (p. 199). Teachers sometimes blamed parents for not taking a more active role in their children's schooling.

Wendy Driver, like Melanie, struggled in school. Her mother was a secretary who kept a close eye on her daughter's schoolwork, listened to her read, went to conferences, and signed all official papers promptly. She was confident that the school knew what was best for her daughter. "Her report card—as long as it's not spelling and reading—spelling and reading are like F's. And they keep telling me not to worry, because she's in the Special Ed class. But besides that, she does good. I have no behavior problems with her at all" (Lareau, 2003, p. 210).

Wendy's teachers were worried, however. Her regular classroom teacher, Mr. Tier, expressed outrage that Wendy didn't know how to read yet and that her mother hadn't demanded that the school do something about it. Wendy was referred for special education, but the referral "fell through the cracks," which Lareau found was more common in poorer neighborhood schools than wealthier ones. Mr. Tier told Ms. Driver, "I would just try to get Wendy to get an interest in reading. Go to the library, find out the types of things she's interested in, read to her. . . . Because I think Wendy could learn how to read" (Lareau, 2003, p. 212). In contrast, Wendy's reading resource teacher, Mr. Johnson, thought she had a "phobia" about reading and that she should repeat the kinds of reading-readiness steps she had had in kindergarten and first grade. Mr. Tier thought Wendy should be in special education full time and repeat fourth grade; Mr. Johnson thought she should go on to fifth grade. So many failures to dialogue here—Ms. Driver did not share her insights with either teacher, Mr. Tier and Mr. Johnson did not agree, and, again, no one asked Wendy.

Dialogue was also impossible in poor and working-class families in Lareau's study when parents feared the school would report them and authorities would take their children away for what they perceived as neglect or physical abuse. Mr. and Mrs. Yanelli worked as a house painter and a house cleaner, respectively, in a European American, working-class neighborhood. Their son, Little Billy, got in trouble frequently at school and at home; his mother reported having to discipline him with a belt about once a week.

In spite of how hard it was to hear reports of her son's misbehavior (believe me, I've been there!), Ms. Yanelli went to parent–teacher conferences. After one, she admitted, "I didn't get to talk about the things that I wanted to talk about . . . I'm not very professional. I can't use the words I want to use. Just because they are professional doesn't (voice drops) mean that they are so smart" (Lareau, 2003, p. 228). Ms. Yanelli eventually saw the school counselor because she felt "pushed" to do so. Her fears seemed justified. "The therapist that day . . . he says well you realize that me being a therapist and working for the state or whatever that if I find out you're beating your child that I have to report that" (p. 221). The Yanellis talked openly about hating the school and the principal. Their biggest fear was that the school would turn them in for child abuse and the state would take Little Billy away.

When our family moved to Georgia, corporal punishment was still used to discipline children. When I wrote a letter asking that my children not be hit, I was, I'm sure, seen as a difficult and lax parent. When my youngest got in trouble for attending an activity he hadn't signed up for, his principal called me and asked in her sweet southern drawl, "What in the world can we do to punish Paul? I just can't think of anything because we always paddle children who break the rules. Now what can we do to help that young man be more responsible in the future?" I assured her I'd take care of it at home.

Social mores change—paddling is expected; paddling is child abuse—and parents and teachers who find themselves with differing philosophies have trouble entering into dialogue. Parents who do not have the social standing I did usually lose the debate, sometimes with disastrous results.

Communicating About Special-Education Referral

Jawanza Kunjufu (2005), an educational consultant with African American Images, pointed out that these results are especially devastating for African American males in *Keeping Black Boys Out of Special Education*. He presented an all-too-common scenario. The parent, often poor or working class, gets a letter like the following (Kunjufu pp. 119–120):

> Dear Parent:
>   I am very concerned about _____'s ability to function in school. . . . [He] is unable to maintain attention or remain seated for more than a few minutes. His excessive movement and impulsivity . . . are extremely disruptive

and have a strong negative impact on his ability to achieve. . . . We request your attendance at an IEP (Individualized Education Plan) meeting to determine the next step.

The next step is a meeting, often scheduled during the mother's workday. Kunjufu (2005) asked, "Can you imagine how she must feel when she enters the room and the professional team is sitting around the table with their papers? She knows she has been talked about. She knows that the decision has been made, her child has already been placed, and her appearance is purely a formality" (p. 121). African American parents' concerns are supported by statistics: Compared with European American females, their sons are 3.26 times more likely to labeled mentally retarded, 2.34 more likely to be placed in LD classrooms, and 5.52 times more likely to be placed in classrooms for students with emotional disturbances (p. 21).

Kunjufu (2005) is writing to African American parents. He is very direct about what they can do to help their children be successful—how to help them with homework, monitor and discuss with children what they see and hear on television and in rap music, and deal with peer pressure. He is also an advocate for parents, with advice including the following (p. 134):

- Do not feel rushed in the IEP meeting. Do not make any decisions or sign any document unless you are absolutely sure that this is the right approach to take for your son or daughter. In fact, wait 24 hours before making a decision. Take the IEP document to someone you trust for review.
- Do not attend the meeting by yourself.
- Ask the principal for a list of parents who have attended IEPs over the past 12 months so you can network with them and strategize.
- Ask the principal which teachers in the school make the most referrals into special education. Make sure your child is not placed in those classrooms. (Kunjufu noted earlier that 20% of teachers in America make 80% of the referrals.)

Sigh. It's hard, isn't it? We all—teachers and parents and principals and grandmothers—want our children to learn, to feel confident, to develop their talents. But we have such a hard time getting past our roles—advocate, educator, parent-who-has-known-this-child-since-birth, teacher-who-sees-this-child-every-day. We all think we *know* what is best. That sometimes keeps us from *doing* what is best. As a parent of a child who was referred for special services, I know that parents need to know their rights and that Kunjufu's advice is very sound. As a teacher, I feel the adversarial nature of the advice. As an advocate for dialogue among children, their parents, and their teachers, I see potential for dialogue only if parents, teachers, and educational consultants all come to the table with equal voices. Only then can we make the best decisions for our children.

LEARNING THROUGH DIALOGUE

That's what Aric's parents and teachers did—they came together. Tina Murray (Leifield & Murray, 1995) was a strong advocate for her son, Aric, to be educated in a regular-education classroom in his neighborhood school; the "official" voices of the school continuously tried to have Aric transferred to a special-education setting outside of his neighborhood where the school was designed to accommodate children with physical disabilities, including those who, like Aric, had cerebral palsy. But Aric's family did not want him in a segregated facility—they wanted "understanding, equality, and normalcy" (p. 238). In many of their interactions, they, like so many parents of students with special needs, felt they were advocating *for* their child *against* the educational system. For example, Aric's first-grade teacher stated at the end of the year that he hadn't made progress in work involving "visual and motor skills, reading, writing, cutting and coloring. Aric is very limited in those areas" (p. 251). She did not mention his progress or his strengths. Fortunately, Aric's parents did recognize his progress and strengths, so he was not retained.

In second grade, Aric's teacher entered into dialogue with him and with his parents. She made him a full member of her classroom and became a joint problem-solver with Tina. She learned from Aric and Tina how Aric learned best and adjusted her teaching so he could learn. She gave tests orally, took dictation of his story for the young authors' contest, and most of all she respected Tina's expertise as a parent. Aric thrived in her classroom, learning far more than he had in previous years. His parents learned that teachers can be supportive partners in their child's education, that they didn't always have to be fighting against the school, and that teachers can also offer great insights into their child as a learner. That year, there was dialogue.

Dialogue is the foundation of creating welcoming schools and family–child–teacher partnerships, especially when teachers and families do not share the same culture. Cristina Igoa, a teacher of immigrant children from many different countries and herself an immigrant, wrote an excellent book that I recommend to anyone teaching students new to the United States. In *The Inner World of the Immigrant Child*, Igoa (1995) describes how she learned not only from her students but from their families. One example of important dialogue involved a 10-year-old girl who came to Igoa's classroom from refugee camps in Afghanistan. She had never attended school. Igoa agonized over where to start: Should she teach her to read in her native Farsi first or in English? "I only have one year with her before the school system will move her along, ready or not," Igoa wrote in her teaching journal. "Must the decision be made on the basis of life survival or from the theory handed to us by the district that one 'learns a second language through the medium of the first'?" (p. 169). She decided to visit the home—she made regular home visits. Here is her account:

> Her father seemed desperate. He was struggling to learn English from a dictionary so he could find a job. He wanted her to learn English, too, so she could help the family. I decided to move into English and kept the door open for her to learn Farsi in time. When I visited her home a third time, she was thrilled. She jumped up and down and said, "I can read. I can read." (p. 169)

Igoa and the father made a difficult decision together, through dialogue. Igoa noted other instances where dialogue in the home directly influenced children's learning. For example, a father from Fiji watched as Igoa tested his son's reading, writing, and math after dinner one evening. Seeing for himself that his child was falling behind, the father began to help him at home, and the boy began making progress. In several other cases, Igoa witnessed children making fun of their parents who could not read or write, or who did not speak fluent English. This is a common "cultural split" for immigrant children between the school and larger society's emphasis on English and their home language. Igoa was able to do some "cultural intervention": "I spoke with each child in the presence of the parents and showed the child how much I respected the wisdom of the parents and how much he or she could learn from them" (p. 128). She was trying to restore dialogue between children and parents.

Action Opportunity: For the next week, think about Freire's challenge to dialogue and observe interactions with others. On a notecard, list examples of interactions where dialogue occurred on one side and, on the other side, where there was a failure to dialogue. When your group meets again, share stories of dialogue successes and failures. Here's what my card might have looked like this week:

Successful Dialogue

- hearing the fear behind an elderly friend's accusation of neglect
- negotiating with Lew about watching bowl game or a movie
- figuring out a budget alternative for a grant proposal

Failed Dialogue

- discussing "political will" at a community meeting on poverty
- listening to grandchildren discuss "If I had one wish" (7-year-old Grace: world peace; 4-year-old Luke: a trampoline; Grace is thoroughly disgusted with her brother)
- getting the late charge removed from my credit card

CHAPTER 6

Inviting Dialogue
at the Conference Table

Shane Rayburn was leading his 3rd graders in a graphing activity when he was called to the office. He had a new student, could he come meet the parents? The principal introduced them. "Well, Mr. and Mrs. Michaels, this is Mr. Rayburn. He will be Travis's teacher. He has a background in special education and will work well with Travis."

Mrs. Michaels, clutching her purse, stopped him before they left the office. "This little boy is the most precious human in my life. He is just the neatest person I know. He has endured so much already. Be nice to him please. Can you help him?"

"Oh yes, of course, yeah, he'll be fine. Trust me," Shane assured them, wishing he could assure himself. A memory of "failing" his brother came, unbidden. Twelve-year-old Shane, so good at learning, was "playing school" to study for a test. His younger brother Christopher started erasing his notes,

82

taunting him to come play. Shane had been livid. It was one of many events that divided the brothers—Christopher resisted anything related to school. Now here Shane was, a teacher, with another family's "Christopher."

"Travis has had some difficult years," Mrs. Michaels said, glancing at her husband. "Travis is like every other child. He likes to play and loves sports. He just has a hard time learning."

Mr. Michaels added, "Please let us know if we can do anything to help at home. I mean we have bought copies of the district reading books and workbooks. . . . We'll do anything to help. We pray that he will learn better and better every day."

Shane nodded, sensing the pain and urgency in these parents. He remembered his parents purchasing extra workbooks, hiring tutors, spending hours helping his brother with homework—trying to help his brother "catch up." He replied, "I know I have a lot to learn from you and Travis. Let's plan to have coffee soon. Then we could talk about Travis and your experiences and all that has occurred before now. Maybe that would help you and me, and in turn Travis."

The Michaels exchanged glances—this was different—and then handed Shane a folder. "Here's a bunch of papers, school reports, and testing results," Mrs. Michaels explained. "You might want to look at them. We have learned to, well, just keep it all in perspective. We know a different Travis than the one on those pages."

Shane took the folder, knowing he would file it without looking at it until he had done his own assessment of Travis. He knew that the Travis he wanted to get to know did not exist in that folder, just as the Christopher he knew and loved was never the child the schools portrayed him to be in conferences with his parents.

(Rayburn, 2003, pp. 77–89)

This informal conference set the tone, the first of many conferences from the next informal chat over coffee to the formal IEP conference later that year between Shane and the Michaelses. It is also the first sighting of some of the ghosts that accompany every teacher and every parent at every conference, whether they are formal parent–teacher or IEP (Individualized Education Plan) conferences, or informal phone calls or chats at the classroom door.

PARENT AND TEACHER CONFERENCES—GHOSTS AT THE TABLE

You sit at the conference table—mom and/or dad, or two moms or dads, or grandpa, and the teacher. But you are not alone. You are accompanied by "ancestral figures." Sara Lawrence-Lightfoot (2003), a Harvard professor (and parent) who studied parents' and teachers' perspectives on the traditional parent–teacher conference, called these often-unexplored histories "ghosts in the classroom." She told about a father who, as he was leaving an otherwise unremarkable conference, blurted out, "That same thing happened to me in fifth grade, and I swear it is not going to happen to my child!" Lawrence-Lightfoot commented, "His passion exploded in defense of his child and in self-defense of the child he was" (p. 3).

Earlier we told and wrote school stories; our ghosts reside in those stories. Some are friendly ghosts of schooldays past: the teacher who helped you win the spelling bee, your grandpa who showed your report card to all his friends at the Coffee Corner, the principal who read the poem you wrote over the intercom, your eighth-grade soccer coach. Others are more menacing: the teacher who read test scores out loud when she handed back papers, the gymnastics coach who told your mom you had no real talent, your dad who whipped you for a D in math on your fourth-grade report card. Every time parents and teachers encounter one another in the classroom, their conversations are shaped by their own stories and by broader cultural and historical narratives that inform their identities, their values, and their sense of place in the world (Lawrence-Lightfoot, 2003).

Listen to the ghosts who showed up at the table in Lawrence-Lightfoot's study of parent–teacher conferences.

Andrea Brown, a Montessori preschool teacher, grew up in a small segregated town in Pennsylvania in a loving family. "The message I got from all of these people who surrounded me was that I was special," Brown recalled. "But my mother was cautious, tentative. . . . On the one hand, I always felt special, beloved . . . on the other hand, I was not quite good enough" (p. 10). While her "very black" father provided "optimism and unfettered love," her mother, who was biracial, was acutely aware of the racism in society and schools. Andrea felt the pressure to perform better than her White peers. Sometimes even that was not good enough; although she had the highest grade point average in her high school, an academic award went to a blond, blue-eyed classmate. Andrea recalled a lovely ghost, her Latin teacher, who whispered to her, "We all know who really deserved that award today" (p. 14). As Andrea told her story to Lawrence-Lightfoot, she realized that her experiences shaped the relationships she created with children and families. She did not want children to feel they must earn her love or families, her approval.

Parents bring schooling ghosts with them as well. Meet Parent A, whose ghosts twirled her in the air singing, "You got all As!" after parent conferences. Meet Parent B, whose ghosts berated him for being lazy. And what about Parent C, whose ghosts whisper to him in soft Spanish tones about a very different way of schooling than the one he is trying to figure out in the United States? Meet Parent D, Paul Holland.

Paul Holland, an African American executive whose children attended a "progressive" private school in Seattle, did not make the connection between his father's advocacy for him and his advocacy for his own son, Stephen, until he told this story to Lawrence-Lightfoot (2003). When Paul was in sixth grade in a working-class public school, his class had a math open house. In her letter inviting parents, the teacher wrote on Paul's that he was doing fourth-grade math. He knew she was wrong; he and his father, James, who was taking night courses, both had an aptitude for math and often did homework together, challenging each other. Paul did not give the letter to his parents, which enraged his teacher and brought him punishment at home. His parents took off work to come to the open house— the only parents to attend. The teacher had the "top math group" work problems on the board; finally, she called on Paul.

> But before the teacher could question him, James rose up, strode to the front of the room, grabbed the math book out of the teacher's hand, and turned to the most difficult problems in the back of the book. When the teacher protested that the class had not yet covered that material, James ignored her and read the questions to his son. Paul stood at the board, quickly working the advanced questions and getting every single one of them perfectly right. . . . The teacher stood there stunned and silent. Finally, she found her voice. "Paul has never, ever done any of these problems before in this classroom," she said softly. "Well, " responded James, "you've never challenged him." (Lawrence-Lightfoot, 2003, p. 26)

Lawrence-Lightfoot commented, "Now, thirty years later, Paul is standing up in front of me in his office, his arms spread wide, crowing like Muhammad Ali. 'The next day my status in the class was transformed!'" (p. 26).

This powerful ghost story haunts Paul at every conference, although he did not realize it until he told it. Many ghosts, like Paul's, drag heavy historical chains of low expectations, chains Lawrence-Lightfoot (2003) explored in terms of "inequalities and entitlements" that haunt teachers as well as parents. When a middle-class African American principal in an elite private school was "confronted by the angry upper-class white parents" who disagreed with a decision, she reported feeling like a slave being disciplined by the master, "a servant who was being yelled at for not following their orders" (p. 37). We drag these heavy chains of discrimination sometimes without realizing the old scripts that we play out or that someone else might feel they are playing out because of our words or actions. It helps to name our ghosts, to tell the story, to see the nods of understanding and empathy from others. Maybe then we'll be able to make connections between our past experiences and what we bring to the parent–teacher conference table.

LET THE LEARNER LEAD
PARENT–TEACHER–STUDENT CONFERENCES

A teacher who was the product of an exclusive private school, Molly Rose remembered hating when her parents went to parent–teacher conferences.

> I was a very hardworking, ambitious student, and I always wanted to do well in the eyes of the teacher. . . . So I'd wait up until my folks arrived home, because all I wanted to hear was what the teacher said about me. . . . I felt as if the adults were talking behind my back. (Lawrence-Lightfoot, 2003, p. 23)

Guess what Molly did when she became a teacher? She invited students to be part of the conference. So did Sandy Sanders, my children's second-grade teacher. Sandy prepared the children to present their own work, to go over their accomplishments, and to explain areas where they needed further work. These were the best conferences I ever attended. I wish I had thought to do the same years earlier when I taught kindergarten.

Molly explained that she wanted "children to have a big voice at the center of the ritual, and . . . to be the primary interpreters of their own experience" (p. 23). Molly involved her students in every aspect of the three-way conferences because "in learning how to gather the evidence, make informed judgments, and report their self-evaluations to their parents and teacher, they develop the skills of documentation and discernment" (p. 91). Talk about teaching critical thinking skills—and these were 6-year-olds. Students kept portfolios of their work and self-evaluations, including checklists for reading, writing, math, social studies, and personal growth. Early in the year, Molly read the items on the checklist to the children in small groups as they looked at their work; by the end of the year, they could read the checklists themselves as they marked *M* (most of the time), *S* (some of the time), and *N* (not yet). While Molly shared tales of a few "disastrous" conferences, the overwhelming majority were highly successful in both empowering the students and informing their parents. "It is such a sight to behold, to see this little kid taking charge, explaining his work, and making informed and clear judgments about his progress," Molly explained (p. 96). Parents told her they had never heard their child speak with such authority; Molly described the children and the conferences as "thoughtful, reflective, and honest" as the first graders set goals and evaluated their progress.

There is a particular challenge—and perhaps an even greater need—in including students with special needs in conferences. Carol Steele, who coordinated a high school alternative program for "students who have successfully failed the school system" (Lawrence-Lightfoot, 2003, p. 166), used frequent conferences, sent daily e-mails to parents, and tried to have students involved in conferences. However, she noted, "It is very hard to get kids to come to these meetings. No matter how hard you try to be fair and welcoming, they tend to regard these parent-teacher conferences as put-down sessions" (p. 171). One student refused to come to the meeting in person but did agree to talk with each participant at the table by cell phone!

Action Opportunity: Discuss what parents, teachers, and students might gain by including students in conferences. What are the challenges? How does including students fit with your curriculum, depending on what kind of standards, materials, and instructional processes you use? What are the pros and cons of some teachers versus the whole school moving in this direction? Who is already involving students in conferences that could serve as a resource? How would you prepare yourselves? How would you prepare your students?

LET EVIDENCE SUPPORT DIALOGUE

Concrete evidence enables dialogue. Whether it is a formal portfolio or an array of student work spread out on the table, it is crucial that parents "see" their child as a learner. The evidence may be carefully selected writing, daily work, projects, and tests (but not *just* tests). Evidence may include artifacts such as photographs of children creating a map of where their favorite book characters live, audiotapes of reading the same story at different points in the year, video clips of a poetry slam. Students may include self-evaluation; parents may also comment and evaluate progress.

Artifacts often prompt stories from the child, the family member, or the teacher. Teachers who share anecdotes with parents show them something important about their child as a learner (Lawrence-Lightfoot, 2003). When our son Luke had been in a Montessori preschool for several months, we had a conference with his teacher. Mr. McReynolds described in detail the joy Luke took in caring for the dog, goat, chickens, and other animals during outside time. He then commented, in a gentle but serious tone, "But sometimes when I ask him to do something, Luke gets this look in his eye— I don't know how to describe it—it's like I'm a little afraid of what he might do next. So far he's always done what I've asked, but there is always that moment." We knew that look, and we knew this teacher both understood and cared about our son.

Evidence of Learning in Various Settings

If the child is receiving instruction from more than one teacher, such as a specialist in learning disability or hearing impairment, a joint conference is highly beneficial, especially if the teachers have been working together as a team. While this is required for students with an IEP, it does not always happen in a way that encourages dialogue. Fania White, who is both a teacher and a mother, felt that her son's teachers had "labeled him a loser, and sealed his fate":

> This is a kid who is super disorganized, who has a hard time remembering to carry his backpack from class to class, and is terrible at managing transitions . . . and here are teachers who refuse to help him figure this stuff out so he can have a chance of being successful. Lord have mercy! Pity the poor kid who has any learning disabilities. (Lawrence-Lightfoot, 2003, p. 147)

Fania obviously dreaded parent–teacher conferences. As the mother of a child with a learning disability, I have shards of memory—some pieces that still cut, others that provide clear visions of plans that supported my son. Luke could not learn math facts but excelled in science and technology. At a conference with his classroom teacher, Ms. Shaw, and Ms. Beats, who taught students with learning difficulties, we discussed Luke's abilities, progress, and frustrations. My husband (a special educator) and I feared that Luke would feel like he was not a capable learner. In fact, several weeks before the conference, he had come home from school one day and said accusingly, "I'm special ed, aren't I." That memory shard still stabs. We had worked hard, his teachers and parents, to explain that everyone learned differently, that Ms. Beats was helping him with the hard parts (math), and the usual things parents say when their children are receiving special services. However, in an announcement over the school PA system, someone called "all special-education teachers" to a meeting and then read their names. Luke was devastated.

The teachers heard us in that conference, and I truly believe they felt the pain we felt as we told this story. Ms. Beats suggested that we also attend to Luke's strengths. We decided together with the gifted teacher that Luke would be included in a unit on computers with the gifted students. He wasn't "officially" gifted, but they recognized that he was indeed gifted in the area of technology. He needed to show his competence. This conference was an example of what special educator Tom Skrtic (1991) called "adhocracy" rather than bureaucracy. In a bureaucracy, many decisions are made by default, relying on standardized procedures (e.g., IQ below 70 = mentally handicapped; reading level below 2.1 = retention). An adhocracy relies instead on collaboration by teachers and parents in dialogue. We acted out of love for Luke, with faith in each other and hope for Luke's future, and with humility that none of us had "the right answer." With that foundation, and with evidence from both home and school that was respected by all, we applied critical thinking to create a unique solution for one particular child.

Evidence of learning may come from other teachers or adults who know the learner. If the child has a gift in art or music or physical education, or is working as an assistant in the library, invite that teacher for the conference. These teachers cannot go to every conference of every child, but they are rarely invited to any. What does that say about what we value?

Evidence in Portfolios

Portfolios are a kind of evidence that often goes far beyond "cold" test scores. One of the reasons many teachers use portfolios as part of their assessment is because they facilitate communication with children and their families. Sometimes teachers collect student work in portfolios; more often, teachers lead students in selecting and reflecting on developing their own portfolios.

Teachers often involve parents in the portfolio process: reading the portfolio together at home, showing the portfolio during parent conferences, perhaps having parents evaluate progress along with the teacher and the student. But here is an interesting twist—in the Intergenerational Literacy Project (ILP) in Chelsea, Massachusetts, families developed home–school portfolios and brought them to conferences. Isn't that a great idea—parents documenting their children's literacy learning at home and sharing the portfolio with teachers? We might think, "These must be highly educated parents who are very comfortable advocating for their children." That was not the case; 60% of the parents in the ILP had lived in the United States less than 5 years (Paratore, 2001). The families spoke 23 different languages and came from 46 different countries.

During their classes at the ILP center, parents learned how to document their children's literacy learning outside of school. In one discussion of the purposes of a family literacy portfolio, parents said the process might help them "see the child's progress," "collect memories," and "learn together." Further, they decided it could be useful "to show the teacher what we are doing at home with our children" (Paratore, 2001, p. 93). Parents collected drawings, stories, lists, letters, and other writing their children did; they also kept an observation log (e.g., reading a sign to a younger child).

Parents brought this documentation to their ILP classes to discuss with each other. At one such session, Paratore (2001) reported:

> First Nubia shared, telling us about the book she read. . . . Then . . . Nubia shared the birthday card her son made for his father. Then Marie Louise shared Kelvin's drawings. . . . Graciela commented that it looked like he was drawing shapes. Roxana shared next about what she did with her nephew. . . . She showed the board book she read and made the noises and people in the class laughed. . . . Marta shared a cereal box entry form that Brenda filled out. (p. 93)

These sharing sessions were tremendously important. They gave parents a weekly forum for discussing and getting feedback on their children's literacy development and confidence in talking about the artifacts and activities. Confidence was essential for the second aspect of the project: sharing the portfolios with teachers.

To prepare for sharing the portfolios, parents read short articles about parent–teacher conferences, raised questions, and role-played what they would do during the conference. They decided it was important to be on time, be prepared (including writing down what they wanted to talk about), ask to share the portfolio, and let the teacher know they were willing to communicate regularly and help their children at home. Teachers also prepared in three after-school seminars where they read about home–school partnerships, learned about the portfolios some families were keeping, and talked about how they might use the parent–teacher conference in a different way: to learn from parents as well as to tell parents what they knew. Paratore (2001) reported that the conversation during the conference was generally friendly and collaborative: Parents and teachers used the portfolio artifacts to build on and reinforce the other's point of view. The practice of validating or confirming what was said was reciprocal—teachers affirmed parents' beliefs and understandings, and parents affirmed teachers' beliefs and understandings.

For example, Paratore (2001) included part of a conference in which the teacher shared work samples from the classroom, showing how Gina had learned to write her name. Later in the conference, the mother presented her daughter's home portfolio:

> *Parent*: So, I went to the bank. Then when I was in the front cashing a check, well, she made a transaction. [Mother displays a withdrawal slip and mother and teacher both laugh].

> *Teacher*: Yeah! Her name is here, her name from left to right!
> *Parent*: So here, she took out one hundred dollars. [They laugh.] (p. 96)

The parent can contribute evidence of learning in other settings; for example, playing soccer, making change in the family store, learning the bus schedule. This is most likely to happen when the teacher invites such contributions, but sometimes parents need to demonstrate their child's abilities. When we had the first conference with our son Paul's kindergarten teacher, she explained that he wasn't very good at following directions because he had been in that Montessori preschool, where children could do whatever they wanted. She did not know Paul could read. I was sorely tempted to go out in the hall, get my child, and hand him a book.

Preparing for conferences is ongoing and involves three highly specialized skills, according to Lawrence-Lightfoot (2003). She discussed these as skills teachers need to develop, but in the context of the partnerships we've been exploring in this book, it seems to me that these are skills that parents and other caregivers will want to develop as well. All of us who are making decisions on behalf of children need to develop the following:

1. the art of observation (so you better understand the learner),
2. detailed documentation (so you can share that understanding with each other),
3. listening "to really hear the voices and perspectives of parents." (p. 105)

This sounds a lot like genuine dialogue to me.

Action Opportunity: Discuss how you might hone these three skills. Use a movie clip, student work samples, or some other object to practice and discuss your skills of observation. What systems of documentation can you share with each other? How could you role-play "listening to really hear"?

Engaging in dialogue is one of the most difficult goals we can set for ourselves as parents and teachers. Parent–teacher (and ideally parent–teacher–student) conferences are the one time a year set aside for this dialogue to take place, but too often it does not—"We have only 11 minutes because the last meeting ran over," "I'd like to stay longer, but Jamie's little brother is out in the hall coughing his head off," "I really have to go over this psychologist's report with you," "You really don't understand how much homework is interfering with our family life." And then there are the ghosts.

I hope this chapter has given you some ways of thinking about the conferences at your school and perhaps opened a dialogue among teachers, parents, administrators, and students. I think we can all get better at them. But we can't rely on them. We have to create opportunities for dialogue all year long, as we'll see in the next chapter.

CHAPTER 7

Creating Dialogue Throughout the Year

"Welcome to Stepford School's Open House. We are so happy to see so many moms and dads with us tonight—we especially love to see those dads! Boys and girls, we're going to ask you to take your mom and dad to your room in a few minutes to see all the exciting things you've been learning.

"But first, I want to invite you all to become active in your child's school life. We are very proud of our parent involvement here at Stepford: We have the highest number of parents who come to conferences and PTA meetings in the whole district—and guess what—we also have the highest test scores! Of course, that's also because you read to your children and help them with their homework every night—well, okay, *almost* every night. Boys and girls, give your moms and dads a big thank-you for caring.

"We have so many other opportunities for parent involvement. We need room mothers for every classroom to bring treats for our Halloween, Valentine's,

Christmas, and Easter parties—oh, excuse me, we're supposed to call those
"winter" and "spring" parties now [*knowing wink*]. And dads, we have several
Stepford Saturdays during the year when you can help us keep this beautiful
school a point of pride in this lovely neighborhood—bring your paint brushes,
hammers, and muscles. We have so many fun family events—Friday mornings
we have Doughnuts for Dads, Muffins for Moms, and this year—Granola for
Grandparents! And you'll earn Stepford Sawbucks every time you walk in these
doors, because we *value* parent involvement and we want to reward you for
caring about your child. Now as you go to your children's rooms, don't forget to
sign in—we know parent involvement COUNTS here at Stepford!"

Who felt affirmed and welcomed and part of the Stepford School family
at that open house? Who felt awkward? Who felt excluded? Who felt belittled?

OPEN HOUSE: WHAT DO OUR WORDS SAY?

Okay, here's where I have to apologize to all the principals I know. I
have attended 39 public school open houses (3 children × 13 years) and
never heard this speech. But I have heard each assumption: assumptions
about gender roles, about mom-and-dad families, about supposedly shared
religious beliefs, about job flexibility, about literacy levels, and about what's
important to children's learning in school-defined parental involvement.
How do parents feel when schools "welcome" them? What do they hear,
and fail to hear, that includes or excludes them?

Debbie Williams, an African American teacher in an urban elementary
school in Philadelphia, understands how important communication is; she
contacts all families before school begins to establish year-long partnerships
and is quite aware of the language she uses with parents. It is more informal, so as not to separate her from families. "Look, meet me the first day
so I can let you know what I'm gonna be all about" she tells parents (Bartoli,
2001). This respectful stance builds bridges; children as well as their parents see their family's language as valid communication.

Building relationships with families means respecting them—their
language, values, struggles, insights, culture, and family structure. Al, a
Puerto Rican father who is raising three sons with his partner Richard,
expressed how frustrating it is when schools and society make assumptions about families. Al and Richard both wanted to be actively involved
in their children's education. However, family configuration and cultural
tradition in their New York City neighborhood both created barriers:

> In Puerto Rican and Hispanic [education systems], the mother is much more
> involved than the father. So we're the oddity. First of all, there is no mother,

and secondly, two daddies. . . . And the school doesn't get people ready for that. They don't even deal with the issue of single parents, much less gay or lesbian parents. (Casper & Schultz, 1999, p. 68)

Families new to the United States may also feel unwelcome at that all-important first school event. ESOL teacher Carmen Urdanivia-English was concerned that her students and their families, primarily Mexican immigrants working in the poultry industry, would not feel welcome in her school. At a faculty meeting that sadly could have been held in many parts of our country, two teachers expressed their strong conviction that if Mexicans come to America, they should learn English. In her teaching journal (Urdanivia-English, 2003), she recorded two events that confirmed her fears.

At the August open house, a confusing event for many Hispanic families, Urdanivia-English posted registration requirements in Spanish on the front office window. "A few minutes later," she reported, "I noticed that the sign was down. Puzzled, I went to the principal who said that he had to take it down due to complaints from parents that a language other than English was being used in the school. If we wanted to post a sign in Spanish, they reportedly said, we had to post it in English first" (p. 189). In a similar incident, an angry parent took a bilingual communication (for parents of ESOL children) to the superintendent. In the future, administrators suggested, Urdanivia-English should write the English version first, then the Spanish—if not "English only," then at least "English first"! She refused "in a symbolic act of standing for the culture of the parents and mine, as well as for their right to communications in their home language" (p. 189).

The next year, Urdanivia-English moved to another school to work with a new principal. Attendance at PTO meetings by Hispanic parents had been low for many years. Committed to creating an inclusive and welcoming school, the principal initiated the use of a bilingual agenda along with simultaneous translation of the discussion and questions not only from English to Spanish, but also from Spanish to English, encouraging Hispanic parents to participate in making decisions during meetings. However, Urdanivia-English (2003) reported, "Soon the school began to hear complaints that the meetings were taking too long, and that the school could provide a written summary of key points for Hispanic parents to read instead of translating on the spot" (p. 38).

However, true to his convictions, the principal continued to hold bilingual meetings, send all communication in both English and Spanish, provide a translator when parents visited the school, and make all parents feel welcome and valued. Urdanivia-English (2003) documented the transformation in Hispanic parental involvement.

At our first PTO meeting, only one Hispanic and about five Anglo parents attended, but the second meeting drew more Spanish-speaking people. . . . The parents were also very much interested in helping their children to learn and achieve, as attested by the large numbers who attended meetings about parenting (92 parents) and homework (78 parents), by their interactions with homeroom teachers when I translated for them . . . , and by their responses to adult classes to learn English. (pp. 38–39)

Spoken words, body language, written communication—our words speak volumes about who we are and who we see others as being. As educators and family members, we have opportunities to include or exclude. We can be Stepford Schools, assuming everyone is alike and conforming to our model of "good parents," or we can be dynamic, evolving, welcoming communities for all learners, all families.

Action Opportunity: Write a "welcome" speech for your next school open house that welcomes everyone into the school family.

SCHOOL-BASED FAMILY INVOLVEMENT PROJECTS

While much of this book focuses on one-to-one relationships of teachers and families and on how families support learning in their homes, there are many excellent examples of opportunities that take place in schools. Remember the research on parent involvement that led to increased student achievement discussed in the Introduction? It was opportunities that engaged children and families in academic endeavors in a trusting relationship with teachers, opportunities like the Intergenerational Literacy Project, Family Literacy Nights, and the Albany Literacy Lab, all of which we'll discuss in the following sections.

Parents as Classroom Storybook Readers

Jean Paratore and her colleagues at Boston University and in the Chelsea (Massachusetts) Public Schools collaborated to create the Intergenerational Literacy Project (ILP) to support primarily immigrant parents in becoming bilingual and biliterate, and to help parents support their children as successful learners at home and in school. In its first 10 years (1989–1999) the

ILP served 1,330 adults (mothers, fathers, grandparents, aunts, uncles, siblings, and others) and 3,535 children. The program has been highly successful in terms of parental attendance, parental interaction with their children around literacy activities at home, and the development of parents' own reading and writing for personal goals. In addition, parents developed ways of reading, writing, and talking with their children and their children's teachers that greatly enhanced children's learning at home and in school.

As parents learned ways of reading with their children at home, some of them began reading in classrooms—their children's room or in some cases other classrooms. Parents chose the book they wanted to read, some written in English and some in Spanish (the largest category of home language). Parents always worked with ILP staff to prepare for the storybook readings; together they previewed the book, practiced reading it aloud, and discussed and practiced read-aloud strategies. These included helping children make predictions, posing questions during reading, encouraging students to join in on repetitive or predictable text, and asking children to retell the story. One teacher commented, "It was exciting to have one of the children's mothers read to my students, I'm sure it will inspire other youngsters to go home and invite their parents to do the same" (Paratore, 2001, p. 91). Before leaving, the parent gave the class several small copies of the "big book" they had read together so children could read on their own. Afterwards, the parent met with her or his ILP "coach" for feedback and suggestions for the next session.

When parents saw how interactive the children at school were during the storybook reading, they began to encourage more interaction during home reading. Paratore's (2001) analysis of audiotaped parent–child home read-alouds showed that "their work in the classroom led them to challenge their own children to engage in what they believed to be new and difficult tasks, and they often found their children to be more capable than they had believed" (p. 91). Parents also learned about American schools—so different from the schools most of them had attended—and the culture of the classrooms in which they read. One mother commented:

> I never saw a class like that before. All of the children were doing different things, and they were all having fun, but they were learning. When I first came in, I thought this is not good, it is not school, but I saw that the children were learning and I think that it's good. (Paratore, 2001, p. 92)

Teachers and children also learned. They were able to see parents who were still learning English as capable and enthusiastic storybook readers. One teacher noted:

The parent kept the students involved by encouraging participation in iden-
tifying pictures and colors. As the story progressed, the students were iden-
tifying the pictures and colors without first being asked. . . . She encouraged
responses from the students as to what parts of the story they enjoyed.
(Paratore, 2001, p. 92)

Family Literacy Nights

In the southern tip of Texas in the Brownsville and Los Fresnos communities, schools are places where families share stories. Dolores Perez
(2005) is a fifth-grade teacher as well as a teacher consultant with the Sabal
Palms Writing Project (SPWP). Like many of the National Writing Projects
across the country, SPWP is deeply committed to "establish[ing] conversations between the home and the school not only to help our students
achieve academic success, but to keep alive their families' pride in and
ownership of their culture and community" (p. 26). Perez and her colleagues began with Family Literacy Nights where teachers, students, and
family members gathered to share their writing.

In this Mexican American community where many family members
did not feel they "belonged" in schools, teachers knew they needed to plan
carefully to create an inviting environment. They developed six guidelines:

1. Make the event festive, inviting, and nonthreatening by advertis-
    ing it in Spanish and English with invitations that do not look like
    the usual communication from school.
2. Embrace parents, teachers, and students by having a greeting com-
    mittee who genuinely welcome everyone at the door, showing them
    where to go.
3. Establish a climate that allows for mutual respect for all stories
    shared.
4. Encourage participants to write from the heart and in the language
    of their choice, honoring the *dichos,* or proverb, "*Quien habla dos
    lenguas vale por dos*" (One who speaks two language is worth two
    people).
5. Provide transcribers for nonwriters, including young children and
    others who are not comfortable with writing.
6. Use prompts that encourage participants to write about what they
    know best. Perez (2005) gave several examples, including the
    following:

    *   What would you like your child to know about your family's
        country of origin?
    *   Map and write about the places where your family has traveled.

- Pick something that is of great value to you and write about it (families brought special objects with them, or selected something from their purses with "sentimental meaning"—a photo, perhaps)
- Write about the best advice your parents ever gave you.
- Write about a favorite "*dicho*," or proverb, and tell what it means to you. Perez included several, such as "*Lo que se aprende en la cuna, siempre dura*" (What is learned in the cradle lasts forever) and "*En la union esta la fuerza*" (In unity there is strength).

Teachers who organized the literacy events in several middle schools shared a goal—"to introduce and nurture the concepts of equity and respect for diverse backgrounds, opinions, and voices. We have worked to respect, preserve, and validate the identities, language and culture of our students and all those who participate" (Perez, 2005, p. 26). What a shift from schools where children are punished for speaking Spanish at school, where parents are told not to speak Spanish at home, and where the purpose of schooling is to "Americanize" children, leaving their "old" cultures behind.

Encouraged by many well-attended Literacy Nights, the SPWP formed a partnership with the Poinsettia community in Brownsville to sponsor a writing group that met to write and share stories. In this more intimate setting, the participants wrote about challenges of limited incomes, isolation in a new country, and working hard so their children could have a better future. One woman shared that she had never had a doll because it was a luxury her family could not afford. Her daughter, who had heard her mother read this story, surprised her mother at the next meeting of the writing group by giving her a doll. Perez (2005) concluded:

> Little did anyone know how profoundly families, students, and teachers would be affected. In many cases, long-lost stories dealing with culture, language, history, spirituality, and family values and customs were resurrected. Not only did parents and students connect with each other, but the link between the family and the school was all the more solidified. (p. 27)

Action Opportunity: In thinking about your school (elementary, middle, or high school), what kinds of ongoing (as opposed to one-time) opportunities might be most beneficial to your extended learning community? Parents reading aloud to children? Family writing and sharing workshops? What are you doing now that draws families in that you might modify for more regular involvement of adults and children learning together?

Albany Literacy Lab

The third example is a school-based, teacher-to-child tutoring program with a strong parent connection. Cheryl Dozier, Peter Johnston, and Rebecca Rogers (2006) designed their University of Albany Literacy Lab (ALL) to engage children as well as their families. With a focus on critical literacy, teachers who study at ALL help students think critically about texts and contexts, authority and agency, prejudice and power in the lives of book characters and in their own lives. The goal at ALL is not only to accelerate literacy learning but also to help students connect literacy to their own lives, their communities, and the larger society. Teachers develop multiple pathways to ongoing communication with families, including taking photographs that document students' literate lives and integrating them into the curriculum, collecting family stories, dialoguing in family journals, making home visits, and attending community events.

Jennifer Grand, an ALL grad, invited parents of her middle school students into the Parent and Teacher Book Group. She didn't teach "parenting skills," or ask parents to get their children to comply with school rules, or even to sign reading logs. She invited them to be part of the literate lives of their children. Parents and teachers selected, read, and discussed adolescent literature so they could talk about books with their kids over the dinner table, brainstormed ways of engaging both avid and reluctant readers, evaluated the appropriateness of controversial books for their own children, and enjoyed reading and discussing literature as equal participants in the book club.

Sometimes we "feel so all alone," especially when we see a child struggling. As teachers, we search for the right approach to unlock the complex process. As parents and grandparents, we sit for hours over homework, purchase Hooked on Phonics, and enroll our children in private centers that promise miraculous results. Retha Brown, a grandparent whose grandson Marcus participated in ALL, did not feel she was alone anymore:

> The tutors have communicated with my family in many ways. I liked the e-mails the best. I've also used journals and family stories where I put stories on a tape recorder. The tutors got to know a lot about Marcus with the pictures they took and the pictures we sent in. That gave an opportunity to find out the things that he liked. . . . I think I've taught the tutors that I'm supportive, that parents can be right there with their children every step of the way. We worked together. . . . As a parent, you reinforce and help at home what they're learning here. We work along with you guys. It's a team thing. (Dozier et al., 2006, p. 177)

Involving family members in the ways we've focused on in this book pays dividends for everyone. Marcus, a nonreader who became a reader through his participation in ALL, could barely contain his enthusiasm for his newfound love. "Grandma, you got time? Papa, you got time? I want to read to you" (Dozier et al., 2006).

DIALOGUE ABOUT STUDENT LEARNING

There are—or should be—opportunities for dialogue about student learning throughout the year. Gail Thompson (2004), author of *Through Ebony Eyes: What Teachers Need to Know but Are Afraid to Ask About African American Students*, surveyed and talked with hundreds of teachers and parents of African American middle and high school students. Miscommunication, misunderstanding, and mistrust marked many encounters. One mother, Deborah, recounted how advocacy for her child became adversarial.

Deborah's daughter was born prematurely, and doctors told her repeatedly that she would not live and that they should not attempt to resuscitate her. Deborah fought for her daughter's life. She lived, and although she had mild cerebral palsy, she was identified as intellectually gifted. Deborah was very involved in her daughter's school, serving as room mother and library volunteer twice a week.

When her daughter, the only African American child in the class, was in third grade, she brought home excellent grades in most classes, but a C in math. Deborah began working with her daughter at home and hired a tutor; she also requested a conference with the teacher. The teacher agreed to have the classroom aide, who was there to assist the child because of her special needs, help her three days a week for 15 minutes with math. Three months later, the child brought home another report card with similar grades. Deborah learned that the extra help never happened; the teacher told her that "the aide was too busy filing papers and planning a whale-watching field trip" (Thompson, 2004, p. 231). Deborah again asked for the accommodation, which was clearly appropriate for her child. Again, the teacher promised, although reluctantly. Again, nothing happened. There was no trust, no respect, no honesty in this failed parent–teacher relationship. There was no dialogue.

Thompson's book is a must-read for many reasons, including a cultural memoir chapter in which she tells of her poverty-stricken and abusive childhood, including abuse from teachers who "hated Black children" (p. 120). But she also had a teacher who saved her, a young White woman who "took a personal interest in our lives" (p. 120).

It is painful but important for those of us who are educators to hear the stories of parents like Deborah. Carmen Urdanivia-English (2003), the ESOL teacher we met earlier, told another story:

It is a cold January morning and I am on hall duty. Mrs. Lynch walks towards me. "Carmen, we will go ahead and start the meeting now. Could you please call the parent and let him know that we cannot wait?" asks the teacher, evidently disturbed by the parent's tardiness. I look at my watch. "It's only 7:15 a.m.," I say. "Yes, but we have to go to class. We agreed to meet at 7:15 to accommodate the needs of this parent, but we cannot just wait until he shows up," she replies.

I call the father, a member of our parent group, and his daughter tells me that he has already left home. As I walk in the room, the teachers in the Student Support Team (SST) are already discussing the child [Luis]. The homeroom teacher briefs the team on the child's difficulties, asking for my perceptions as his ESOL teacher. About three minutes later, a neatly dressed, small man shows up in the door.

"Siga, Señor Fernando," I invite him. *"Buenos días,"* he rushes into the room, his face slightly red and short of breath. "Good morning," answer the teachers at once, three out of five stretching their lips in forced smiles. . . .

Constraints imposed by job responsibilities affect teachers' ability to interact with parents, as happens this morning, when the teachers are apprehensive at delaying their return to their classrooms. In addition, stereotypes about Hispanic parents that portray them as not concerned about being on time increase the teachers' anxieties.

I struggle to soften the words delivered by some of my co-workers as I interpret for the parent, but I cannot shield him from non-verbal messages while he quietly listens to our discussion. "The child is defiant. He does not even look at Mrs. Turner when she is talking to him. *That's very disrespectful,*" says one of the teachers, as I share that some of such attitudes could be cultural. "Yes, but unless the child answers, there is no way for Mrs. Turner to assess his learning," she retorts.

Hostility escalates when the parent hesitates on the group's recommendation to retain the child at the end of the school year. As I inform him about his rights to decide about the education of his son, Fernando continues to withhold an immediate answer and I suggest that he let us know his decision later. Instead, he asks us what can he do at home to help his child, and we advise him to read with him every day and to talk about homework and school. Toward the end of the meeting, the team lays down possible dates and times for follow-up, consulting with Fernando. When he suggests that we meet early in the morning, two of the teachers mumble to me, "Be sure you tell him to be here on time. We cannot just sit down and wait because we have children in our rooms."

I do not have to translate. With a low voice, he says in Spanish that because he is the supervisor of a group of workers about 75 miles from town, he had to drive all of them to work in the morning and then come back for the meeting. Fernando's humble, measured reply has a tremendous impact on the group, as anger and criticism turn into understanding and empathy. Now we do not know what to say, how to apologize to him. (pp. 180–187)

Later, when Carmen talked with Fernando about the meeting, he told her how he had been influenced by being in the parent group Carmen had organized where they discussed the "rules of the game" for parental involvement in the U.S. "I thought that never, that is that they didn't . . . , that we shouldn't—we shouldn't ask questions of teachers. Never before did I come to school. And (my children) used to say, 'No, man. I'll not take you (to school). You are very ugly' (laughter). However, I have learned that one must ask, (we need to) talk about the things we think are not right. I learned that at the meetings you hosted, because I heard someone saying that one day. And so, I said, 'Look, one can also decide, it's a parent's right.' Because before (the meetings) someone would say 'Your son will go to this place (program)' and I (would say), 'That's fine. You are the teachers,' I used to say. 'You decide.' Now I know, we can also make decisions."

Concha Delgado-Gaitan (2004) has worked with and studied Latino families and educators for over 25 years. She reported the following testimonial, translated from Spanish, to illustrate the importance of regular communication. Mrs. Sosa's son Mario was in Ms. Mora's third grade at the time:

> As parents we get together weekly . . . at the community center and discuss our children's education. It was in meetings with this group of parents that I learned how important it was for me to communicate with my son's teacher the entire time even when he was doing well. . . . At first, I didn't think that his teacher paid attention to Mario, and she didn't think I cared either. But we were willing to talk, and find out where we differed and where we agreed. What has helped me most is that the teacher has taken the time to help me learn how to help Mario. . . . Mario has shown some real progress since his teacher and I have been communicating more often. . . . Now he stays occupied with his schoolwork and he actually finishes it because I think he knows that his teacher and I agree on what's good for him. (pp. 24–25)

CULTURAL UNDERSTANDING, CROSS-CULTURAL DIALOGUE

The largest minority group in the United States is Latinos, at 13% according to the Bureau of the Census (2000), yet there may be the greatest communication gap between educators and Latino parents in many schools due to unfamiliarity with language, culture, and educational norms and expectations on the parts of both teachers and parents. There are many Latino cultures, including but not limited to "Mexican immigrant, Mexican American, Chicano, Central American, Latin American, Puerto Rican, and Cuban" (Delgado-Gaitan, 2004). Within each of these cultural groups there are multiple other areas of identity and circumstance, from family structure to professions as varied as migrant worker to governor. While acknowledging individual, family, and cultural differences, Delgado-Gaitan found in her 25 years of research in various Latino communities that many families shared the following values:

> *Respeto.* Respect for education and educators.
> *Respetar a otros.* Strong sense of mutual respect in relationships.
> *Ser buen educado.* An emphasis on discipline and proper behavior.
> *Compadrazgo.* The relationship between parents and godparents, translating into co-parenting. (p. 3)

As discussed elsewhere in this book, there is overwhelming evidence that most Latino families value education for their children; indeed, that is why many families immigrate to the United States. However, if parents are not familiar with school terms or cannot read the assignment in English, they may have trouble helping children with homework—something schools often see as indicators of families valuing education. Delgado-Gaitan (2004) provided a poignant example of what happened when one child did not understand an assignment and her mother tried to help. In a typical doing-her-homework-while-mom-fixes-dinner American family scene, Norma asked her mother (in Spanish), "What's a character?" They looked together at the book cover, and her mother pointed to the illustrator's name. "I think that this is the person you need. . . . Wait, this isn't it." They skipped this question and moved on to "author's name," eventually selecting the book's title, *Zoro*, to fill in the blank. Norma's teacher may have thought her parents were unwilling to help her when in fact her mother tried very hard to do so.

There are opportunities related to these values for genuine dialogue. For example, if a child is behaving well, a parent may not understand a teacher's concern that she is lagging in math. In an example from Valdés (1996), a teacher and a parent who both valued education failed to communicate. Mrs. Lockley recommended that Saul be retained in first grade, angering his mother, Velma, who had had no indication prior to Mrs. Lockley's letter that he was failing. For Mrs. Lockley, part of Saul's problem was the "fact" that his parents were not "involved" in his education. She pointed to lack of communication with Saul's mother "as evidence of both disinterest and lack of involvement" (p. 4). However, Velma valued education highly and did what she thought would help. Velma had enrolled in a mail-order book club and had asked for help interpreting Saul's report cards. Mrs. Lockley didn't know of these efforts, but she did know that Velma rarely came to the school or called, so she decided that Velma wasn't involved.

Delgado-Gaitan (2004) offered several concrete suggestions that schools have found effective for supporting Latino parents in helping their children with homework. You might discuss them in terms of the cultures of families in your school.

- Run spots on Spanish radio stations with advice on helping with homework.
- Set up a Homework Hotline in English and Spanish.
- Establish a school or district Homework Center where parents and/ or bilingual teachers could help children after school.
- Reach out to Latino churches and social or civic groups in the school district to help inform parents about meetings or workshops. Delgado-Gaitan illustrated how important monthly meetings with a teacher (and in one case a principal) were for parents to discuss what their children were learning and how they could help.
- Hold bilingual focus group discussions for parents—co-facilitated by a bilingual teacher, counselor, or administrator and a parent—to learn their concerns about homework. Together you could do the following:

    Create a list of phone numbers for parents to call for assistance in helping their children with homework (their child's teacher, another parent, etc.).
    Encourage parents who may not read English to ask their children to explain their work when they have finished it. This helps the child understand on a deeper level (or see where he or she doesn't understand) and informs the parent about what the child is learning.
    Arrange for tutoring and/or help older students form study groups.

Parents teaching parents. Parents teaching teachers. Teachers teaching parents what they want to know. Dialogue that is based on mutual respect. These are powerful settings for the kind of parent involvement that makes a genuine difference in a child's life as a learner.

CHAPTER 8

Engaging Families

> We cannot know a culture unless we know the people whose spirit keeps it strong.
>
> (Buley–Meissner, 2002, p. 323)

First-grade teacher Betty Shockley, second-grade teacher Barbara Michalove, and I (1993) studied the children we worried about most. As we followed six children for 4 years of elementary school, we became acutely aware of how little we knew about the children's families, how little the families knew about what their children were doing in school, and how little genuine communication occurred. Betty designed and Barbara adapted a set of parallel practices to connect home and school literacy learning (Shockley, Michalove, & Allen, 1995). Those practices included a letter from parents/ caregivers about their child, home reading journals, oral and written family stories, learning albums, and adult literacy conversations. Listen to how Betty described two of these components are described:

> You should have seen Brandon the morning Betty read his mother's story to the class. He positioned himself in the middle of his classmates as they huddled expectantly on the floor around her. . . . Brandon curled down over his knees, placing his hands on top of his head as if to keep his body from popping up uncontrollably like a jack-in-the-box whose spring was wound too tight. As Betty read aloud his mother's contribution to our class book of family stories, he could not contain his excitement. He giggled in expectation, leaped up laughing at times, and at the conclusion sighed, "I can't believe my mom wrote that!"
>
> You should have seen Betty each morning as she read each home-school reader response journal. She too had a difficult time containing her joy as she saw children and parents building relationships around books. Invariably the stack of tablets would reveal some new insights recorded by either the children or the parents . . . [such as] the following entry from Brandon's journal in which his mother gained a glimpse of her efficacy as a parent. . . .
>
> February 12
>
> Book: The cow That Went Oink
>
> How Brandon saw this story interested me greatly. Brandon said that it was a sad story because the other animals laughed at the cow and the pig because they were different. He said he was glad because it ended the way it did. I've taught Brandon *never* to laugh at anyone because they are different, and to never laugh at anyone's misfortune. I'm glad that he applied my teachings to this story. It shows that he "really" takes to heart the things I say. (Shockley, Michalove, & Allen, 1995, p. 3)

"TELL ME ABOUT YOUR CHILD"

Betty and Barbara began with the parents' perspectives of their own children, inviting them to "tell me about your child." Betty's invitation was a lined piece of paper with this invitation at the top: "Hello! Welcome to first grade! Parents have homework first! Please write and tell me about your child." Barbara's invitation in second grade (with the same children and families) said, "Dear Parents, It's always exciting to start a new school year with a new group of students. I look forward to working with your child. Please take a few moments to tell me about your child. Thanks, Barbara Michalove."

Every family wrote back. Who could resist such an invitation?

Parents in this lower-income, predominantly African American neighborhood poured out their hopes and humor, information and insights, advice and anxieties about what their children were like and what they hoped school would be like for their children. One parent confided, "Torry's confidence in himself is not the greatest. However, he will overcome this with love and attention." Another bragged, "Ashley can find anything around the house and make it into something beautiful and interesting" (Shockley et al., 1995, p. 19). Debbie and Jerry Anderson wrote:

> Our son, Adrian Jerome Anderson, is the highlight of our life. . . . He's interested in learning and trying new things. He's very independent, attentive, and gregarious. . . . He has been taught to respect others and obey grown-ups, but occasionally he tries to see how far he can go over the line. A mere reminder is all he needs to put him back on the right track. . . . The best thing about Adrian is that he is a very warm and lovable person. His father and I love him very much and he knows it. . . . If we had to describe Adrian with one word, that word be special because that's what he is to us. (p. 31)

This theme—our child is unique, special, and very dear to us—echoed across all the letters. Janice Barnett's pride in her daughter was equally evident:

> Lakendra Echols is very witty. She likes to go to movies, and she like to go to the mall especially the toy store. And most of all she likes to help with the house work. Washing dishes the most. Lakendra like to be my big girl; she's very outspoken about what's she feel. Me and Lakendra have no secrets from each other. I can trust my big girl and she can count on me. She's my little star. (p. 41)

HOME READING JOURNALS

Teachers and families kept this dialogue going all year in journals the children took home three (first grade) or two (second grade) times a week, along with books from the classroom libraries. Parents or others in the family sustained a remarkable commitment to read with their children, talk about the books, and write together in the journals. One child told Betty, "My mom read . . . while I was taking a bath. Yeah, I was in the tub and she was sitting on the toilet—the lid was down—and reading to me" (Shockley et al., 1995, p. 20). Betty and Barbara honored the families' investment of time by responding to every entry. This was important not only to parents but also to their children. LaToya's mother told Betty, "She comes home with the journal and starts asking me, 'What did she say? What did she say?'" (p. 20).

"What they said" was based on the principle of reciprocity between families and teachers. Betty and Barbara knew that reciprocal relationships—we must learn from each other in order to be the adult support system for this child's learning and development—took great time and care to build. As Moll, Amanti, Neff, and Gonzáles (1992) wrote, mutual trust "is reestablished or confirmed with each exchange" (p. 134). It can also be threatened or destroyed in a careless exchange. Consequently, Betty and Barbara were very careful about their invitation and their responses.

At the beginning of first grade, Betty invited families to take an important part in their children's literacy development:

> In our class, reading and writing are viewed as very connected. . . . We read many books each day and write like real writers every day. Our homework practices also reflect this style of learning. Each night . . . your child will bring a book and a reading journal home . . . please read WITH your child every night. Remember, your child will be choosing the book s/he takes home, so on occasion the book may be too difficult for your child to read independently. You can help by asking your child if she wants to read the book herself or if she'd rather you read it to her. Then use the journal to write down her responses to the reading. Sometimes YOU may want to write me about the selection yourself and model for your child ways to think about what we read, or sometimes you may want to have your child dictate to you his interpretations, or sometimes your child may want to do it all by himself. What I'm trying to say is relax—enjoy this time together—there's no one right way. (Shockley et al., 1995, p. 20)

Families took her at her word, establishing their own styles and uses of the journal. They talked about stories, illustrations, information they learned, insights about their children's literacy development, and sometimes the concerns that fill every family's life (Shockley, 1993). This extended written communication, not about enlisting parents to solve discipline problems or to sign agendas or permission slips, established deep relationships. It also supported emerging readers and writers at home as well as at school in ways neither teacher nor parent could have accomplished alone.

Debbie, Adrian's mother, wrote about a very thick book on bears her son brought home early in first grade. She explained:

> Because we didn't get home until 6:45, we were not able to go into great detail with the book . . . [however,] Adrian was most intrigued by the fact that bears can run up to 40 miles per hour for a short distance. We used the speed limit on North Avenue to compare the rate of speed of the bears. (Shockley et al., 1995, p. 32)

Debbie often used books to teach Adrian about family values—a book about an aardvark who got glasses became a lesson on not making fun of

people, and Goldilocks reinforced the message that children should listen
to their parents. When Debbie and Adrian read *Galimoto* (Williams, 1991)
in second grade, Debbie wrote in the journal, "This book shows what hard
work and determination can do for you. I asked Adrian what he thought
the moral of the story was and his response was 'don't let someone tell you
what you can't do.'"

Barbara responded the next day:

> Good for you, Adrian. I think you're right, and be sure not to let anybody tell
> you that you can't do something that you know you can! I also like the set-
> ting of this story. Last year we had a visitor from Somalia. . . . He told us
> all the children make galimotos [cars] out of odds and ends. (Shockley et al.,
> 1995, p. 35)

The journals became places for expressing family values, beliefs, and
practices. Adrian's parents expected correct spelling on most words by
second grade and had him recopy some of his entries into the journal; Barbara honored this expectation, even though she took a more developmen-
tal approach to spelling in the classroom. Mary, LaToya's mom, particularly
appreciated books that gave them the opportunity to talk about their African American heritage:

> LaToya read, "Follow the Drinking Gourd." I enjoyed this book with LaToya.
> I am glad she is finding books to read about her own people. She asked me a
> lot of questions about slaves and white people and why they hate each other,
> and why she should be proud to be black. She had so many questions it took
> us 1½ hours to read this book and for me to explain things to her. Mary (p. 72)

Parents gradually began sharing the responsibility for writing in the
journals with their children, sometimes at the gentle urging of Betty or
Barbara. In October of second grade, Adrian wrote, "In a Town There Was
a young Boy who was a Woodcutter. He Saw that Town and Said he was
not afraid of Nothing. The Morale of the story is How Big you are Doesn't
Mean the Bigger the Badest" (p. 35). The teachers responded to each entry,
whether written by a child or an adult. They had intimate conversations
about books, reading, writing, school, and other important everyday aspects of being part of a shared home and school learning community.

Journals often became a site of collaborative literacy support. Parents
suggested that teachers send home books that were harder, or easier, or
had more words. Teachers suggested that parents try reading a difficult
book to the child first, then listening to the child read. They discussed complexities, such as the difficulty a child could have comprehending when

spending so much energy on decoding. Many of these parents had not completed high school, but because they were invited into a genuine dialogue where all opinions and suggestions were respected, parents as well as teachers could concentrate on the child and what might be the next steps in his or her journey toward literacy.

For example, Janice and Lakendra read together every night, and Janice took a keen interest in Lakendra's development. Here are some excerpts from their journal (Shockley et al., 1995) that demonstrate her determination:

> *Janice*: In the story I Can Fly Lakendra did very good. Her reading was very good. And maybe she's ready to move on to a few more words. I mean a book with a few more words. If you think so also. (9/30)
> *Betty*: I agree. She can read more difficult books but like everybody, young readers enjoy reading things that are easy for them too. (10/1)
> *Janice*: Ms. Shockley, In the story of the Haloween Performance, Lakendra seem to have some problems with many of the words. Maybe she get a story with too many difficult words for her right now. But still I enjoyed her reading. Thank You. Janice Barnett (10/2)
> *Betty*: When you get ready to read together each night, you might begin by asking Lakendra—Do you want to read your book to me or do you want me to read to you? Sometimes after you read even a more difficult book she may ask to read it after you. Let her be the leader. One of the most important things about sharing books together is talking about them together. Thanks. (10/3)
> *Janice*: Lakendra was very excited about the books she chose to read to me. So excited she read them over and over again. And I was so pleased. Maybe last night she did want me to read the story to her I don't know but I will ask her from now on. Because she was a little upset that she didn't know a lot of the words. And I don't ever want her to feel pressured. Thanks. Janice Barnett (10/3) (pp. 42–43)

A serendipitous result of the year-long written dialogue was the tremendous support teachers and parents provided for each other. They encouraged and thanked and empathized. They problem-solved and consoled and celebrated. For example, Janice thanked Betty and Barbara regularly in the journals; she wrote at the end of one entry, "Thanks for yal great methods of teaching." In turn, the teachers often encouraged parents, as when Barbara wrote, "Janice, Lakendra is doing well with reading and writing in class too. Thanks for taking the time to listen to her read. It really makes a difference" (p. 46). Parents as well as teachers recognized their efficacy as teachers. It is almost as rare for teachers as it is for parents to get such positive feedback on a regular basis.

ORAL AND WRITTEN FAMILY STORIES

Betty and Barbara demonstrated respect by accepting both the content and form of whatever family members wrote in the journals. Many who might not have viewed themselves as writers took great risks not only by writing several times a week but also by contributing to family storybooks. Family stories were another way of bringing home cultures to the center of the classroom curriculum.

The morning routine in Betty's room included oral storytelling, complete with the storyteller's stool and karaoke microphone. Students rendered everything from household events to tall tales (not necessarily labeled as such). Children wrote daily, often recording the stories they had told earlier in the day. But the biggest storytelling event of the year was the Family Stories class book. "The invitation was open-ended," Betty emphasized, "and each family wrote something different, from narratives about marriage, birth, death, and religion to poetry and family sayings" (p. 22). My favorite was the exciting story of the home birth of a baby sister—complete with illustration of the "crowning" moment!

Not all stories came in right away; writing stories was an even more public risk. But as several of the children brought their stories to school and read them to the class, more children urged their parents, "Let's write a story about our family!" Eventually, every family had a story in the class book.

One family story began, "What me and my family believes. We believe that Jesus is our lord and savior." What an invitation—to share at school deeply held family beliefs. Janice and Lakendra contributed family sayings that quickly became class favorites:

> When it's raining and the sun is still shining, the devil is beating his
>   wife.
> When it rains, God is crying and when it thunders, God is angry.
> When a black cat crosses the road and goes to the left, it's bad luck,
>   and to the right, it's good luck.
> If you kill a frog, you will stump your toe.
> Open an umbrella in the house, it's bad luck.

In second grade, Barbara held a class meeting about family storybooks. The children were unanimous—they would ask their parents or grandparents to write about "when you were little." Barbara loved the range of stories in the second-grade book, Stories of Our Lives. "Ashley wrote about being attacked by a bulldog, and her mother reminisced about a tire swing in the family oak tree. Greg wrote about a ride at Disneyland; his aunt wrote about moving from California to Georgia. . . . Frances Ward, the instructional aide, told of swallowing a marble as her mother quilted nearby" (p. 22). Barbara wrote a Hanukkah memory.

These books became well-read classroom treasures and public celebrations of families and their stories. In first grade, parents were honored guests at a book-signing party; in second grade, parents read their stories at a parent meeting. The children saw their parents and teachers as readers and authors, enjoying one another's stories and encouraging the next generation of storytellers to continue the tradition.

LEARNING ALBUMS FOR FAMILY, CHILD, AND TEACHER REFLECTIONS

Because family members were so central to their children's learning, Betty and Barbara knew they should be involved in every step of the process, including evaluation. They collected assessments throughout the year in Learning Albums that included the "Tell Me About Your Child" letters, response journals, units of study that the parents and children discussed at home, student writing, and reading assessments. At the end of each year, parents and students reflected on their learning. The information from the first-grade evaluations was quite valuable to Barbara in planning for the children's second-grade experiences. Parents responded at home; students responded at school. The questions were parallel for parent and child—for example, "How did your child learn to read" and "How did you learn to read?"; "Does your child like to write?" and "Do you like to write?"; and "What would you like your child's teacher to do for your child next year?" and "What do you hope second grade will be like?" (Shockley et al., 1995, p. 23)

Parents and children consistently recognized how important parents had been in helping their children become readers and writers. They also believed that reading together at home, talking about the books, and writing in the journals had been an important part of the process. One of many things the parents agreed on was that they wanted to continue the home reading journals—but two times a week instead of three because the children were reading longer books and writing longer entries in second grade!

Adrian's dad, Jerry, a sergeant in the army who was often overseas, wrote one of the longest reflections, emphasizing the importance of the parallel school–home practices:

> We can see a definite change in Adrian. He has gone from dreading going to school to looking forward to the next day. . . . I'd like his teacher to continue

to be creative like his first teachers were. I like the idea of learning outside of the textbook. Learning is fundamental, but it should also be fun. I especially liked the idea of bringing a different book home each night and a journal to write down ideas, concerns, or whatever was on your mind. . . . I liked knowing what and how Adrian was doing in school all year long, not just at parent-teacher conference. (Shockley et al., 1995, p. 37)

LITERACY CONVERSATIONS AT PARENT MEETINGS

Parents met with Betty, Barbara, and me seven times during the second-grade year. At the September meeting, Betty read aloud the draft of an article about the children and families engaging in parallel practices, using their actual names, as they had requested (Shockley, 1993). The eight moms and four dads applauded and were visibly touched. Barbara led a discussion of what the parents wanted their children to learn in second grade and their thoughts on family meetings. As Barbara recounted, "They were very enthusiastic about this opportunity to 'do things together,' 'interact,' [and] 'communicate with the teacher all the time, not just at conferences'" (Shockley et al., 1995, p. 25). Barbara shared the students' list of what they wanted to learn and do that year, including going camping and fishing, studying Australia, going on a dinosaur dig, and going to the zoo and a ballet. Parents were enthusiastic about their children's ideas; many went with the class on a camping trip the next month and contributed to the curriculum in many other ways throughout the year.

Other meetings focused on family memories, making the books for the family stories, sharing what we were reading as adults, and an end-of-year family picnic at a city park that 14 of the 18 families attended. It had been an incredible 2 years, filled with connections—families and teachers, families and children, children and teachers, and readers and books. Most of all, it made a difference to the children. Brandon's mom said it best:

> Ms. Shockley,
>   When you said that we were a "special group because of the 100% participation [in home reading journals]," I felt proud but at the same time a little shocked and a little sad.
>   When I grew up, it was hard for me to get my parents to participate in anything I did in school. That really affected my sense of "worth". I thought I was a burden to my parents. Also, I wasn't really excited about school. I felt if my parents didn't care, why should I? that is why I take the time out with Brandon in helping him with his school work. I want him to get excited about homework [reading and writing in the journals].

I was so glad for the "homework". It gave me the opportunity to be in the "scholastic" part of his learning. I can appreciate it and I feel that it has helped Brandon's learning. I remember when the journals first started I would read to Brandon. Towards the end Brandon read to me. He was eager to learn more words so that he could read more, so he learned!

I think my child is special. I have only one time to raise him and one time to teach him and one time to be a part of his growing up. If I show I care, then maybe he would be that caring parent also. Kathryn Eberhart (p. 27)

There are many aspects of "engaging families" that can be adapted for different ages and different purposes. Teachers at various grade levels have modified home reading journals; in upper grades, students have read the books to themselves or read aloud to parents, then discussed them and written in the journals. Parents and high school students have read and discussed the same novel. Parent-written stories, book-signing parties, families developing curriculum—there are so many aspects of the work of these two remarkable teachers that we can learn from. What I learned from Betty and Barbara was to focus on constantly creating partnerships, not programs. Programs are developed by other people and "implemented." Partnerships are created by all participants.

Action Opportunity: Parents, teachers, what aspects of "engaging families" would be beneficial to your children? What are the opportunities for ongoing communication during the year that focus on the child's learning? How could families be involved in assessment in ways that help the student as a learner? What kind of forum would facilitate sharing family stories? Dream, create, risk, revise. Make it your own.

We'll close with a letter illustrating the power of engaging families. Dennis, a child with many early indicators that he would fail, did not. He had a powerful team in his corner—a teacher who believed in him and parents who accepted her invitation to read and write together all year. In May his mother wrote (Shockley et al., 1995):

Dennis read really good I only told him about 4 or 5 words when he finished reading I clapped my hands and gave him a big kiss on the cheek and told him he did great. He's really becoming a smart child. I was just thinking to myself. If a child has wonderful teacher and wonderful parents that takes up time with him and helps him to read and learn new things he turns out to be a genius. What I think my little Dennis will be someday. (p. 144)

CHAPTER 9

Engaging Families
in Classroom Projects

My mother's earliest memory from China is of hiding in the bushes from Japanese soldiers. Her mother was covering her mouth so they wouldn't be heard. That was her earliest and only memory of her biological mother. She was then given to a woman whom I call my grandmother. This woman also put her in someone else's care when she immigrated to the States. She sent money back, which was supposed to pay for my mother's education. Instead, the woman kept the money and put my mother to work like a child servant or slave.

(Campano, 2007, p. 53)

This moving account by Erica Lee is from an interview with her mother. How much family members have to share about the time, places, politics,

> **Action Opportunity:** Before reading the rest of this chapter, bring to-gether parents and teachers, including those teaching special education, the arts, and physical education as well as media specialists. Brainstorm a list of curriculum topics or units of study you do throughout the year. In what ways might family members be involved directly in student learning?

and events that shaped their lives! In this chapter we'll explore additional ways families can engage in the kind of involvement that matters—as active partners in their children's learning.

WRITING YOUR HERITAGE

Deborah Dixon (1993), a teacher consultant with the South Coast Writing Project and a teacher in an Intensive English Program, developed a sequence of writing activities to help her students explore their cultures as well as develop their writing abilities. She and others have used this sequence successfully with middle school, high school, and college students. While she does not explicitly involve other family members, the sequence is ripe with possibilities for doing so. Dixon's sequence is detailed below, along with my ideas about how to involve families. In other words, I did what I asked you to do in the above Action Opportunity—look at existing curricula and think about where family members might join the circle of learning. My ideas are in italics.

1. Diagram your family tree and include names, places, dates, occupations, religions, important events, and so on. *Students start their research by talking with family members. This kind of assignment has been controversial for many people who worry about issues of divorce, incarceration, adoption, legal status, and other aspects that parents may rightly feel are private. It might be helpful to talk with students about this right to privacy and have them discuss it with their parents. Maybe as a class you can develop ways of representing the family tree that protect such information. The process will be much stronger if teachers and parents and kids develop the guidelines together.*
2. Write a letter or a tribute to one of your ancestors. Dixon's college freshmen read *Notes of a Native Son* by James Baldwin and *In Search*

of Our Mothers' Gardens, in which Alice Walker paid tribute to the poor but highly creative Black women in her family. *I love this idea. It is going to be a stronger piece of writing (and learning) if the student interviews several family members with stories of ancestors. I'd also ask students to discuss these or similar readings with older family members and to think about how their families are similar or dissimilar.*

3. Create a "family crest using words, images, and color to represent [your] ethnic or national origins, . . . traditions, religions, and family occupations," and include a family motto representing "family value, belief, or tradition" (p. 7). *What a great family art project! It gives parents an opportunity to stress what they think is important about their family. If the biological, foster, or adoptive family is not one a student wishes to focus on, then perhaps the student can write about his or her school family, faith family, or sports team family and talk with adults in these community settings.*

4. Describe yourself in terms of what you are learning about your heredity; tell what parts of your personality seem influenced by your cultural heritage. *I think kids of almost any age would get into asking other people to describe them: "Papa, is there anything about me that reminds you of any of our relatives?" "Tía Esperanza, am I like people in the town where you grew up?"*

5. Research "the coming to America of your family or ethnic group, or an historical event one or more of your ancestors did or could have participated in" (p. 20). *Dixon's students used multiple resources from the library; today we'd add electronic resources. For this assignment, family members could do the research side by side with students at a public library (both print and electronic resources), at a community center, or at home. They can "mine" family archives and talk about any photographs, letters, journals, slave records, immigration papers, or newspaper clippings they may have.*

6. Bring an object that "represents some aspect of [your] cultural identity . . . and talk about its significance to [your] family or culture" (p. 29). Dixon has wonderful examples of students performing Basque sheep calls, showing a lace pillowcase a grandmother crocheted, sharing "great-grandmother's wedding ring, a precious symbol of the first woman in her family to be married out of slavery" (p. 30). *This made me think of objects in my house that are special to me that I may never have really shared in any intentional way with my children. My Grandpa Firing was a Norwegian immigrant who was an excellent wood carver. I have a picture of him as a young man, fresh out of the Norwegian navy, in one of his frames. My children passed it every day.*

> *I wonder: Do they know he carved the frame, or how he learned to carve, or how he got from the Norwegian navy to a small town in Illinois?*

7. Listen to and write about music "concerned with problems that can come with honoring the values and traditions of one's cultural community" (p. 30). Dixon used songs from *West Side Story* and *Fiddler on the Roof. There is often a divide—sometimes a stormy one—between generational music choices. Here's an opportunity to have a family conversation about music on neutral terms. The talk shifts from "How can you listen to that (boring, loud, obscene, stupid) music" to "So can you think of a song that comes from our culture or talks about values or events important to us?"*

8. Write about language as political and as "a key to identity (personal and social)" (p. 34). Students in Dixon's classes developed their skills of argumentation around language, debating whether "old" values and traditions in their families and/or cultures should be cherished or ignored. *Engaging students and their families in the study of language can take many forms: interviewing family members about family sayings and traditions, discussing English-only debates, or recording and comparing examples of different word choices and dialects at home and in the media.*

9. Write a position paper on heritage. Dixon poses several possible questions, such as "Is the study of heritage divisive or community building? How does/should/can a multicultural society address the diversity of its population" (p. 40). Her freshmen addressed issues of ethnic labels, Mexicans "stealing" jobs from "Americans," living in two cultures, and the pressure of being a "model minority." One student wrote, "I am only half Asian, but society views me as Asian and therefore I must be academically wise" (p. 41). *I'd ask students of any age to read their drafts out loud to at least one other person in the family and to ask, "Does my argument make sense? Do you agree or disagree? Why? Are there parts that I need clarify?" This is an opportunity for family to be involved in a highly academic task that does not demand advanced reading skills but instead engages the family member in listening, thinking, and discussion with the writer.*

Dixon's (1993) book contains other steps as well as excellent references to poetry, short stories, and other literature to weave throughout the experience. While this extensive and intricate sequence is important for older students, it could be modified for younger ones. The key is that inquiry into a topic of interest to students is also an excellent way of involving families in meaningful work that is both personal and academic.

Students also "write their heritage" in the Life Story Project. Nor, a Hmong American college student, knew little about his family's flight from Laos to the United States. All his parents had told him was that their village had been bombed and they had fled to Thailand and then, 2 years later, they moved to the United States. However, when his teacher, Mary Louise Buley-Meissner (2002), involved him in a Life Story Project, he began to study the history of the Hmong people. He learned that the CIA had recruited them to fight the communists in Vietnam and then reneged on its promise of protection, leaving them to brutal persecution after the fall of Saigon. Nor's family, like thousands of others, tried to survive in the jungles of Laos and Thailand, but his grandmother and a 2-year-old sibling died of starvation. Nor's mother "tied the other children to herself, one in front and one in back, dosing them with opium when there was no other way to keep them quiet" (Buley-Meissner, 2002, p. 327).

Nor did not hear these stories from "interviewing" his parents. "I couldn't ask my parents about the war. I didn't know what to ask, what to find out. I couldn't suddenly start to say, 'What did you go through? How did you feel?'" (Buley-Meissner, 2002, p. 327). However, as he learned the history of the Hmong people, he talked at home about what he was learning. His parents began talking about their experiences. "They're interested. They're surprised. They tell me what they remember, a little at a time" (p. 37). Buley-Meissner emphasized that students should simultaneously be learning from a variety of sources and talking about the information, opinions, and controversies with parents as a springboard for learning about family history.

CREATING FAMILY KEEPSAKES

"Keepsakes" are what Linda Winston (1997) calls the stories children and their families created in the New York City schools in which she conducted workshops. An English and language arts teacher for 10 years in kindergarten through eighth grade, Winston engaged teachers, students, and families in creating family keepsakes. Teachers at Manhattan Country School created Family Study, a social studies program in second grade that reflects the school's racial, cultural, and socioeconomic diversity.

Teachers in Family Study used different strategies to start their keepsake projects, including making quilts and collages. Children often interviewed family members about how they were named, because names "not only define us, they also contain our family histories. Interviewing someone about her name will reveal her family-naming folklore and her family as well" (Winston, 1997, p. 12). Here is one child's story, although it loses much of its power without the rich brown figures in his accompanying drawing:

> A time before I was born, Mom and dad wanted a strong name for me. Mom wanted Christopher, but Dad said, "No. Let's call him Timothy." Grandma Broome wanted a saint's name, so Augustine became my middle name. That was great because it is part of my dad and brother's middle name, Augustus. Now we three have middle names that start with "A." (p. 12)

Family Study also included grandparents and other family elders. Children learned skills of "silent interviewing" (observation) as well as oral history interviewing. The children wrote biographies of these family members and sometimes organized Family Museums with artifacts representing family members. The culminating event was a family potluck where students read and talked about all the family projects they had created. Besides the children's growth as social scientists and writers, there were benefits for the adult family members. "Parents learn more about other families in the school. . . . They also make discoveries about how they are perceived by their children" (Winston, 1997, p. 26).

In Ted Kesler's third-grade classroom, family stories were immigration stories. He met with parents early in the year to plan the study together. Immigration was a natural focus: "The Countries Where We Come From" chart listed Ireland, Czechoslovakia, Israel, Hungary, India, Japan, Trinidad, Dominican Republic, Russia/Ukraine, Brazil, Lithuania, China, and England/Scotland! Children talked about voluntary (immigration for economic, political, and religious reasons) and involuntary (slavery) entry and the increasingly political issues surrounding immigrants. With their parents, they created time lines and family trees, wrote the story of their names, and searched for newspaper articles on immigration. They interviewed family members, read children's literature, and wrote immigrant stories. Ted interviewed his own father in the classroom. He also respected the right of families not to share private information. Winston (1997) attended the presentation Ted's class made with handmade puppets, a photo slide show, and children reading from their original stories of immigrant journeys:

> It isn't often that a group of adults is genuinely moved by a grade school play. However, dramatizations of immigration stories, based on the experiences of the children or their families, are the exception. While there may be some tears throughout the house, the people who aren't crying generally have smiles as wide as the rivers or oceans they've crossed. (p. 70)

Some keepsakes are not written but passed down as family lore has been passed down for generations in some cultures—through storytelling. Kit

Fung invited teachers, children, and families in her school, primarily working-class Chinese families, to tell stories by sharing hers. She told the story of her names (birth name, pet name, school name). In the Chinese tradition, stories often convey moral values. Kit noted, for examples, "A story like 'Den Dai Ching Wu'—'The Frog Who's Looking Up from the Bottom of a Well'— warns about pride and boasting. . . . You think you are so great, but you are only looking up from the bottom of a well" (Winston, 1997, p. 47).

Another teacher, Cheryl Tyler, invited parents to come in once a week to tell stories of their childhoods. As a reporter from the *New York Times* wrote after being invited to one of the storytelling events, these stories "proclaimed the city's human mosaic." The mosaic became a museum the next year—a Family Museum of keepsakes "from wartime army dog tags to baseball cards, bottle tops, and buttons" (Winston, 1997, p. 31). Another year, Cheryl launched a child–parent poetry project. Parents came to a poetry celebration where their children "made the classroom reverberate with joyful sounds as they sang, recited, and dramatized many of the poems they knew," including a finger-snapping version of Eloise Greenfield's "Things" (p. 32). The next month, parents began sharing favorite poems with their children for a collective poetry book, soon a class favorite.

Whether through written stories, oral storytelling, or sharing poetry, all families can contribute—and at the same time preserve—their family keepsakes. In the next section, we'll look at another way to make families central to children's literacy learning.

AUTHORS IN THE CLASSROOM

I love *Authors in the Classroom: A Transformative Education Process* by educators and children's book authors Alma Flor Ada and Isabel Campoy (2004). Every teacher I know who has read it marvels at the way it has, indeed, transformed her or his classroom community. These communities include students, family members, and teachers at all grade levels who express important ideas through poems, stories, photo essays, and books.

The theoretical foundation of *Authors in the Classroom* is rock solid: Ada and Campoy (2004) believe that education has the power to transform lives. Their goal is "Creating a classroom community in which equality, justice and peace are explored in both thought and action" (p. 4). Remember our discussion in Chapter 5 of dialogue and Freire's conditions—love, humility, faith, hope, and critical thinking? Ada and Campoy devote a chapter to fostering dialogue among students, families, and teachers. And remember how we forced ourselves to look at oppression? The authors propose that one way of breaking the cycle of oppression is through writing about and sharing our lives:

When we encourage teachers, students, and parents to empower themselves as authors, we are providing opportunities to listen to and record numerous voices that have gone unheard, lives about which no one has ever written. We are also reaffirming parents' role as educators by inviting them to partake directly of the benefits of print and books, and of the value of recording, producing, and disseminating their experiences. (p. 3)

The authoring process invites variations on the following basic pattern (Ada & Campoy, 2004). I couldn't resist adding a few thoughts (in italics).

1. Read and discuss high-quality children's literature on the topic (e.g., Understanding the Past or Understanding Relationships). *Students, families, and teachers can gather all kinds of texts—news articles, song lyrics, paintings, comic books, poetry, picture books, Internet sites, and so on— "critical literacy text sets" (e.g., http://education.indiana.edu/~langed/faculty/harste/paper.html) that combine both popular culture and school culture.*
2. Share the texts with families. *Students could take them home after discussing in class, parents with flexible schedules could be invited to the classroom, and/or the teacher or school could sponsor Family Authors Nights (or Saturdays, based on family time preferences).*
3. Talk about the theme of the unit, and select one text for in-depth dialogue. *While the authors' themes are broad enough to encompass many interests, I'd encourage conversation among families, students, and teachers to select themes. For example, in my hometown, affordable housing is a critical issue. Developers are purchasing land where mobile home communities live, forcing the inhabitants out, which often means the loss not only of the land but of the homes too old to be moved. A theme of "home" would allow families to explore their own "home" stories as well as the stories of others in the community.*
4. Write your own book or poem, then share it with students and send it home to share with their families.
5. Encourage students and families to create their own poems, photo essays, books, and so on. Ada and Campoy's book has dozens of inspiring examples. Share these with students and families—it is very powerful to see what other children, parents, and grandparents have written. Teachers encourage family members to write in their home language or, if they are not comfortable writing, to tell their children what they want to say so the children can write it down. *Adults in the family could also tape-record the story, proverb, advice, and so on, using a school tape recorder. This way children actually "hear" parent voices in the classroom.*
6. Share the products. Some teachers send home family contributions as they come in, to inspire other adults. Teachers often create class-

room books with contributions from all children and families. Many books are written bilingually, created in the family's home language and then translated into English.
7. Celebrate together. Family events are profoundly moving and educational, as participants reflect on their learning processes and beautiful literary products.

Nina Montepagani, a teacher in Troy, New York, invited parents and caretakers along with her diverse class of English Language Learners to co-author a book on an object with special meaning to each family. She asked questions to help writers think about what to include: "What is the object? What country is it from? What size, color, and shape is it? How did you get the object? . . . Why is this object important to you and your family?" Nina also asked them to draw the object (Ada & Campoy, 2004, p. 74). The invitation resulted in a 100% family response—"a first for me," Nina rejoiced. The class book, *Something Special*, is just that. Here are just a few of the objects:

- A Korean family shared "traditional cloth called Ham Bok in Korea. . . . The color is very bright and wonderful. Also, it is very comfortable" (p. 75).
- A Pakistani family drew a famous mosque.
- A Saudi Arabian family drew a teapot and wrote, "My grandmother give it to me. . . . In our culture we usually drink tea together after meals. And sometimes we meet with our relatives to drink tea and share talking about our life" (p. 75).
- An Algerian family wrote about a medallion with the Hand of Fatima, who was the revered daughter of Muhammed, given to the mother by her grandmother: "It keeps us in touch with our roots, cultural and religious, . . . it will be an honor to give it to my kids" (p. 76).

There are so many ways that families can be a part of the learning community—Are you ready to plan yours?

Action Opportunity: Go back to that list you started at the beginning of the chapter. What ideas can you add? Commit to starting with one collaborative project this year—just one!

CHAPTER 10

Collaborating for a More Just Society

Of all the civil rights for which the world has struggled and fought for 5,000 years, the right to learn is undoubtedly the most fundamental . . . a right to an education so students may judge the world *not as it is*, but *as it might be*.

(DuBois, 1949/1970, p. 230)

Sixth-grader Jason, fifth-grader Pablo, second-grader Kaeli, and their mothers had just presented their research on the Underground Railroad in Iowa at a reading conference. They were part of a research group at Horace Mann Elementary School in Iowa City, parent–kid–teacher investigators (PKTI), who study their community. Jason wrote:

My group worked really well together during the presentation. My mom answered a lot of the questions, but soon I felt comfortable and wanted to answer some questions, too. When I relaxed, our talk felt like it was flowing so well that my mind drifted back to all of my memories of working on the Underground Railroad group. Kaeli, the youngest researcher in my group, had asked the first questions, "What was the Underground Railroad?" and I thought that was so interesting. At first we found a lot of books and read some of them, looked at maps, and—the best part—went on a field trip to see a real Underground Railroad station in Keosauqua, Iowa. We even interviewed my dad, James, because he's an expert on African American history. That was really cool since he was teaching my friends about what happened to my ancestors. He showed us his antique toys, books, and a slave collar he just bought. I felt proud of him because he has a lot of knowledge about history and he is a great father. (Hicks, Montequin, & Hicks, 2000, p. 26)

I love the fact that Jason, his mother, and his teacher wrote this article together (Hicks et al., 2000) and published it in an issue of *Primary Voices* in which other members of PKTI described this unique research group. This project and others like it in this chapter allow us to move from how teachers and family members get to know each other and learn from each other to what they can do together.

PKTI, a diverse group of 35 adults and children, met every other Monday for dinner and high-energy talk about their collaborative research. Families who had lived in Iowa for generations joined those who had moved there recently and whose native languages were Icelandic, Russian, German, Spanish, and Malawi. Students wearing white paper plates with questions they had generated walked around the cafeteria as other students, parents, and teachers decided which research team they wanted to join. They then clipped a clothespin with their name on it to the paper plate, and a team was born.

Together, children and adults in these diverse PKT investigations read books and pamphlets, phoned an antitrust lawyer about toy pricing and mark-ups, searched the Internet for lunch menus at schools around the country, marked a map of Iowa with Underground Railroad stations, interviewed the police chief about local crimes, weighed all the food thrown away in the cafeteria for 3 days, and visited a historic Underground Railroad station. They wrote field notes, drew maps and diagrams, shot photographs, and produced a video "investigative report" on school lunches. They studied the world as it was, and is, and might become.

In this chapter, we ponder collaborations like PKT in which students, families, and educators take democratic action in their schools, communities, and society.

COLLABORATING FOR DEMOCRATIC SCHOOLS

Education is the foundation of our democratic society, so how can schools contribute to making that society more democratic, more just? Carol Edelsky (1999) argued that education *in* a democracy has to be education *for* democracy. In other words, teachers have a responsibility to teach in ways that promote a fair and equitable society, ways that equip students to be active citizens in moving the United States toward democracy in those areas in which we, as adults, have failed. Education for democracy has its roots in social movements, such as the movements for civil rights for African Americans, women, Latinos, people with physical disabilities, and people who are gay, and progressive educational movements, such as the movement for multicultural education (Banks, 1993; Sleeter, 1996).

What opportunities might teachers, students, and family members create to work toward a more just and democratic society? Let's see what others have done.

A Yup'ik Community in Alaska

Rather than being taken over by the Bureau of Indian Affairs, the townspeople of St. Mary's, Alaska, a Yup'ik community of about 500 people, decided to incorporate so they could manage their own educational system. Many other Alaskan communities followed their lead, according to Ray Barnhardt (1990), an educator and anthropologist in rural Alaska. Local control has been key in meeting the district goals of helping students "to preserve and maintain their own cultural identity and language, and to develop the skills and knowledge necessary for successfully dealing with, and living among, other cultures and people" (p. 57).

One way the district is accomplishing this goal is by involving parents and community members democratically in the educational process. They adapted a list of Yup'ik values from one generated by the Inupiat Eskimos in the Northwest Arctic region, to guide all members of the community (Barnhardt, 1990).

> With Guidance and Support from Elders We Must Teach Our Children Yup'ik Values: Love for Children, Respect for Others, Sharing, Humility, Spirituality, Cooperation, Family Roles, Knowledge of Family Tree, Knowledge of Language, Hunter Success, Domestic Skills, Avoid Conflict, Humor, Respect for Tribe, Respect for Land, Respect for Nature. (p. 62)

These values are applied in curriculum development and in community practices. One of my favorites, which I learned about when I visited the Yup'ik village of Toksook Bay, is the beginning-of-school potlatch. In this potlatch, parents present students with pens, pencils, and other symbolic gifts as well as give their advice for the school year. In the spring, students reciprocate by thanking elders for their support during the year and performing Yup'ik songs and dances that they composed at school.

Action Opportunity: Discuss Yup'ik values in relation to your own community values. Which are the same? Which would you delete? Add? Reword? Who isn't "at the table" as you have this discussion? How could you learn their perspectives? What if students interviewed their parents and other elders in their community? Finally, plan beginning-of-school/end-of-school ceremonies that might make sense within the cultures of your community.

PICO and COPLA Community Efforts

There are many effective school–family–community partnerships working toward democratic education; we'll look at the Pacific Institute for Community Organizations (PICO), dedicated to improving students' academic success and increasing educational equity, a cornerstone in a democratic society, by improving communication with teachers, helping high school students stay in school, keeping students' identity strong, and supporting high school students' efforts to graduate and pursue college (Delgado-Gaitan, 2004). PICO brings people of many cultural backgrounds and more than 50 different religious denominations and faith traditions together to improve opportunities, including education, for poor, culturally diverse communities. Their mission statement (http://www.piconetwork.org/) explains that PICO is a national network of faith-based community organizations working to create innovative solutions to problems facing urban, suburban, and rural communities. Since 1972 PICO has successfully worked to increase access to health care, improve public schools, make neighborhoods safer, build affordable housing, redevelop communities, and revitalize democracy. With more than 1,000 member institutions representing 1 million families in 150 cities and 17 states, PICO is one of the largest community-based efforts in the United States.

While I am a strong believer in the separation of church and state in terms of religious practices and doctrine, I believe just as strongly that a coalition of families, educators, and people of all faith communities can be a powerful force for improving education. In PICO, parents meet regularly to discuss issues about their children's well-being and to develop their own leadership abilities and strategies. Families, churches and other community groups, and educators have collaborated to improve educational opportunities for students through initiatives such as comprehensive after-school programming in Gainesville, Florida; handicapped-accessible school playgrounds in Thibodaux, Louisiana; a street-outreach program for youth in Rochester, New York, called Pathways to Peace; and many more.

Delgado-Gaitan (2004) shared one mother's story. Christina moved to Oakland from Mexico. Concerned about her daughter's schooling, she soon joined the local PICO, where other parents helped her develop strategies for advocating for her child. Delgado-Gaitan wrote, "She became acquainted with the good teachers who were willing to help her daughter excel. By the time that her daughter got to middle school, one of her teachers helped her to get a full scholarship to a private girl's school" (p. 115).

While PICO is a multicultural organization, the Comité de Padres Latinos (COPLA) formed in 1985 in Carpinteria, California, specifically to advocate for students by increasing Latino parental involvement in K–12 schools. Workshops are often led by teachers and parents together. For example, in one meeting, two high school English teachers talked with parents about their expectations of students and parents. Then parents asked the teachers about opportunities for their children, many of them still learning the English language, to attend college. They were concerned that the school did not offer college-prep courses in Spanish. As a result of the meeting,

> The teachers and the principal made it clear to the parents that it was possible for Spanish-speaking students to advance into the right classes for college if they took extra English classes in high school, worked with tutors, and worked hard on their own time to learn English. . . . Parent told the teachers and the principal that they wanted their students to receive better counseling about the required courses for college. The parents also emphasized the need for the school to open college-prep courses in Spanish so that Spanish speakers had equal opportunity to attend college. (Delgado-Gaitan, 2004, pp. 123–124)

A Focus on Important Issues

Tackling the real issues in students' lives not only increases motivation and engagement; it can lead to creative solutions. Poor children are five times as likely to have high lead levels in their blood, have twice as many severe (and uncorrected) vision problems, and have three times as many untreated cavities as middle-class children. Asthma is the single largest cause of student absenteeism; poor children not only get asthma more frequently and more severely than middle-class children but are less likely to be able to afford treatment (Rothstein, 2004). How does a kid with a toothache learn? How often are children in your school absent because of asthma? What if parents, educators, and students investigated the effects of such health issues on their own school?

One community—one of the poorest in California—did just that. In Contra Costa County, the average Verde Elementary School (VES) student missed one out of every nine school days. Not surprisingly, given high poverty and absenteeism, VES ranked the lowest of 6, 209 schools on the statewide Academic Performance Index in 2000. When Janice Thompson became principal, she pulled school staff, county agencies (Departments of Employment and Human Services, Health Services, Probation), community organizations, and VES students and their families together to establish the VIP (Verde Involving Parents) program. They assessed the complex problems affecting the children and developed interagency strategies. One was the Integration of County, School, and Community Services to Promote Student Success; so often services are available, but families don't know how to access them. A second was the In-School Support and Celebrations process involving conflict resolution, anger management, and development of problem-solving skills; teachers and parents learned and practiced these strategies with students at school and at home. The third, and perhaps most critical, strategy was Parent-to-Parent Outreach and Assistance, staffed by Family Partners.

Family Partners, all parents of VES children with strong school attendance, helped grandparents, parents, and other caregivers who needed assistance in getting their children to school. They picked up students in their cars or on foot and brought them to school. Once at school, Family Partners called or made home visits to all families of absent or tardy students. The purpose of the calls and visits wasn't to browbeat or threaten parents with jail, as some districts do. Rather, they talked, parent to parent, to find out what was keeping the child from school. They offered their help in contacting the resources needed to address the underlying problems. For example, one student was chronically absent because she had headaches and toothaches. When her mother explained this to the Family Partner, she contacted the Family Service Center's public health nurse, who arranged a dentist's appointment that very day. Once her badly infected teeth were treated, she was able to return to school.

So did it make a difference? You bet it did. The VIP program reduced unexcused absences by a monthly average of 72% during its first year, and Verde students made major gains on the state Academic Performance

Index in 2002 and 2003 (http://www.shcowell.org/grant/Recent_Grants _Richmond.html).

There are excellent examples all over the country of school–community partnerships, many of them working to increase educational equity and access. In a review of more than 100 community-based organizations (CBOs) that were nominated as effective partnerships, Weiss and her colleagues at Harvard's Family Resource Project (2005) identified CBOs that offer successful programs for students placed at risk and English Language Learners. These partnerships, which offer programs before, during, and/ or after school, are housed in schools, in community centers, and at university campuses. Weiss pointed to partnerships such as the Filipino Youth Empowerment Project in Seattle, where 75% of the high school students in the program went on to college, and the Chinatown Service Center in Los Angeles, which provides tutoring and health service in an elementary school. One of the largest partnerships is between the New York City United Way and the Board of Education. They formed the Community Achievement Project in the Schools, facilitating connections among over 100 CBOs and 100 schools.

COLLABORATING FOR A DEMOCRATIC SOCIETY

We move now from how communities can collaborate to help schools to how schools can collaborate with communities to work toward social justice.

The Llano Grande Center for Research and Development

In the southern tip of Texas, teacher Francisco Guajardo at Edcouch-Elsa High School rallied students, alumni, teachers, parents, and other

---

Action Opportunity: Before your next study group meeting, gather data. Ask students and have students ask parents, "What are the most pressing issues in our school or district?" Examine by race, gender, and economic status who is graduating, being retained, taking Advanced Placement courses, enrolled in gifted classes, assigned to behavior or emotional disorder classes, playing sports, and so on. What kind of inquiry and action could you take together?

community members around intertwined goals: (1) Students in this primarily poor, Mexican American community would get the best college educations in the country and (2) students would work with adults to revitalize the community. Guajardo made a compact with the students: They would be prepared for, attend, and succeed in Ivy League and other top colleges; in turn, they would "give back" by returning to the community to mentor and inspire the next generation of students. Through the Llano Grande Center for Research and Development, the students—and the community—are accomplishing these goals.

The context for this collaboration is important. Ninety-one percent of the students' families earn less than $10,000; few parents have high school diplomas. "Approximately 40 percent of Edcouch-Elsa High School students follow the crops with their families. Within a few weeks, the school population can expand or shrink by hundreds of students" (Null, n.d.). When I was in elementary school in Texas, there were children of migrant workers in my class for a few months every year. I never got to know them. I remember the hot flush of shame I felt sitting in my fourth-grade classroom on many occasions as the teacher berated my Mexican American classmates for being stupid and dirty. His unsubtle message: You do not belong. You cannot learn.

Francisco Guajardo is the antithesis of that cruel teacher. He and his colleagues and their community believed in, taught, and mentored students, and more than 80 of them to date have in fact been admitted to prestigious universities. And they have come home—doctors, teachers, business executives—some to stay, some for visits, all to inspire and encourage. How has this remarkably successful process worked? How has Edcouch-Elsa High School moved from a failing school to a state "recognized school" by improving its students' performance on the Texas achievement test?

The Llano Grande Center, which serves nearly 5,000 K–12 students in the area, focuses not only on student achievement but also on community development, documenting cultural traditions and inculcating cultural pride. The center's programs train students to document—through interviews, photography, and other research techniques—the historical contributions of their families and other community members. Students, teachers, parents, alumni, and other community members study community needs, define objectives, and design projects that have helped to revitalize the region's educational, cultural, civic, and economic life. "Teachers and children alike have been inspired by the testimony of devoted, resilient men and women describing, in their own voices, how they have coped with harsh economic and physical challenges while providing for their families" (Null, n.d.). These stories, published in both English and Spanish, are now used as texts by students at all grade levels "who have reworked them into fiction, artistic depictions, and a television documentary which . . . students produced for the local PBS station" (Null, n.d.). Five of the ninth graders were invited to exhibit their photo essays at the Smithsonian in 2000.

The oral history interviews often led to action and an impressive record of grant funding for intergenerational leadership training and school–community projects, as shown in this example:

> Students, teachers, and community . . . held a conference for those who had witnessed or taken part in a walk-out at Edcouch-Elsa High School in the spring of 1968. This pivotal event, protesting discriminatory practices throughout the local school system, hastened the end of "Anglo" dominance in local politics and local schools. . . . Several local educators were influenced and motivated by the walkout and its aftermath. Sharing reminiscences with other area residents as well as with a new, curious, and caring generation has been a way of increasing positive exchanges between communities inside and outside the school walls. (Null, n.d.)

What distinguishes the work of the Llano Grande Center and similar projects is that students and adults are working together for a common purpose. This isn't "parent involvement"—this is collaborative action. There is a shared sense of purpose and mission. Fourth graders and their parents work alongside city council members; high school students publish and broadcast news not as an assignment but as contributing members of their communities; students of all ages have conversations with their parents about the issues that are vital in their community.

The Institute for Democracy, Education, and Access

Many educators and parents have noted that opportunities for parental involvement change, at best, or disappear, at worst, as students enter high school. It is important for students, teachers, and parents to plan together meaningful ways of collaborating that draw on the strengths of each

---

Action Opportunity: If you live in a rural community—or anywhere else, for that matter—you may want to read *Thriving Together: Connecting Rural School Improvement and Community Development* (Boethel, Averett, & Jordan, 2000). This publication from the Southwest Educational Development Laboratory is an excellent resource for planning school–community development projects.

group. An outstanding example of such a collaboration is the 5-week summer seminars sponsored by UCLA's Institute for Democracy, Education, and Access, led by Ernest Morrell (2004). Each year since 1999, students, school and university faculty, and parents from urban schools have designed and conducted collaborative critical research projects. The goals include helping students acquire the tools of academic literacy needed in universities and conducting research that influences policy and promotes educational justice locally and statewide. All seminar topics relate directly to the communities in which the students live, as these examples illustrate:

- Potential of hip-hop music and culture to transform high school literacy curricula
- Different manifestations of student resistance in urban schools
- Impact of teachers' attitudes towards students' home languages on achievement
- Political, social, and educational issues in the 2000 Democratic National Convention (held that summer in Los Angeles)
- California students' educational rights, inequalities, and advocacy
- Urban youth participation in civic life

Research teams of four to five members articulated their own questions; they then collected and analyzed data using surveys, interviews, photography, videography, legal documents, and historical artifacts. They produced PowerPoint presentations, wrote research reports, and presented to groups of educators, politicians, university and school faculty, civil rights attorneys, community activists, and parents. These collaborative inquiries were not "school assignments," and parents were not there simply to sign off on "homework." Parents have become very involved, along with their young scholars, in presenting and writing about the research (Morrell, personal communication, August 4, 2005).

FROM CITIES TO SINGLE CLASSROOMS

While they are not partnerships per se, I think it is worth mentioning what Richard Weissbourd (1996) called "family-friendly cities." The most remarkable example to me was Seattle. In 1986, in his effort to make Seattle a Kids' Place, Mayor Charles Royer *required every agency in the city to include an item that benefited children in its budget*. Wow! In 1990, Mayor Norman Rice continued this commitment by encouraging family-friendly workplaces and the Comprehensive Child Development Program for low-income working families.

Action Opportunity: Call your mayor, tell her or him what Charles Royer did, and say, "Let's make this commitment in _____ (your town). I'll help. Where shall we start?"

Don't think that all collaborations have to be on such a grand scale. Bronx public school teacher Marceline Torres (1998) involved her sixth-grade students in self-selected projects investigating "important questions and concerns about the world in which they live," such as drugs, AIDS, teen pregnancy, and homelessness (p. 59). She also got their parents involved (1) by having students dialogue with their parents in "letters home" and (2) by holding monthly "celebrations" at which students presented their research findings to their parents. Family members became valuable resources; for example, one student interviewed his uncle, who had AIDS, and another got technical information about the disease from her father, who was an X-ray technician.

Vivian Vasquez, a teacher–researcher in Ontario, shows that even very young children can engage in education for democracy at school, community, and global levels. In her multiethnic classroom, 3- to 5-year-old students raised questions deriving from the storybooks Vasquez (2004) read to them, things they heard about on television, and conversations at home. They tackled school, community, and global issues such as these:

- What can we do to help save the rain forests?
- What has happened to the trees that were once in our neighborhood?
- Who is left out of the books we have in our library?
- What can we do to help the Manitoba flood victims?
- How do people become disadvantaged?

During open house, phone conversations, and home visits, Vasquez talked with parents about the critical literacy curriculum she and the students would develop and how important ongoing communication would be. She invited parents to three "open dialogue nights" during the year at which parents viewed what the students called their Learning Wall—pictures, artifacts, and texts that showed everything the children had been investigating. Vasquez (2004) characterized these nights as times where parents "could come in to talk about issues, questions, and comments regarding their child's learning in an informal group setting. This was a social gathering time as well as a time to look at the artifacts that had been posted on our audit trail" (p. 43). Parents became involved in conversations at home about the issues children were studying, including raising funds for the World Wildlife Fund of Canada and boycotting McDonald's, Burger King, and other fast-food companies that manipulate children into buying their food and toys.

One movement in education, academic service learning (ASL), has an established track record of leading to increased student engagement and learning. Academic service learning at its best involves students and teachers in investigating the needs of their community and working with parents and other community leaders to study an issue and take action. There is a solid body of evidence that ASL, done well, can enhance academic achievement (including state tests in Pennsylvania, Michigan, New Hampshire, and Vermont), increase attendance and graduation rates, and help students develop civic dispositions—in other words, students develop both the skills and the inclination to be citizens in a democratic society by helping create it (Billig, 2000).

Parents are sometimes a neglected resource in service learning projects. Here are four examples of ASL that do include parents:

1. Students in one Alameda County, California, classroom planted a garden, studied ecosystems as well as soil and water quality, analyzed nutritional quality and balanced meals, and donated the food to a local homeless shelter. While they learned a great deal, this cycle did little to address the issue of hunger in the community until they took the next step: Students, their parents, and the teacher worked with people at the shelter to plan and plant a community garden at the homeless shelter. Residents now grow their own fresh vegetables.

2. Students, teachers, parents, and community members in another Alameda County school worked with the local Conservation Corps to clean up a polluted creek that ran through the school campus. They studied ecology, the history of species native to the area, safety, and techniques for preserving wilderness areas. Their follow-up studies showed increased life and decreased toxins, findings that they presented to the local water-quality board.

3. In Georgia's White County Intermediate School, students, teachers, parents, and community members worked together to research and restore the dilapidated gravesite of Revolutionary War surgeon Joseph Murdock. Fourth-grade teachers developed lessons incorporating state curriculum objectives in several content areas, including character education. Students generated questions such as: How were people buried 200 years ago? How does this inquiry relate to

our lives today? How can our project become a learning situation for us and the community? Their work grew out of the school's focus on *democratic service learning* (Allen & Thompson, 2005).

4. Fourth and fifth graders in Indian River, Florida, became concerned about their favorite bird, the scrib jay. Because of loss of local habitat, it had become an endangered species. The principal and a teacher brought parents, children, and environmentalists together for weekly strategy sessions to save the scrib jay. Together, they made a presentation to the school board, county commission, a member of Congress, and the secretary of the U.S. Department of the Interior. Through a grant from the U.S. Fish and Wildlife Service, they are working to create a wildlife sanctuary.

If you want to learn more about academic service learning, you might start with some of these websites. Not all include parents—how you can become involved is up to you and your child to figure out as partners!

- Corporation for National & Community Service (Learn and Serve America grants): http://www.learnandserve.org
- National Service-Learning Clearing House: http://servicelearning.org
- Generations United (intergenerational programs throughout the country, some service learning programs): http://www.gu.urg

As this book went to press, I read the most wonderful book, *Black Ants and Buddhists: Thinking Critically and Teaching Differently in Primary Grades.* Teacher Mary Cowhey (2006) collaborates with students, their families, and community leaders and activists to address the issues that constantly arise in her classroom of highly engaged critical thinkers. They didn't just bake

---

Action Opportunity: Invite community leaders to talk with teachers, parents, and students about the most pressing issues in your community. In my community, those issues are affordable housing, the effects of development on the environment, services for homeless people, and a shameful high school graduation rate. Form teams like the ones in the PTKI discussed at the beginning of this chapter to investigate issues and plan civic action.

pies and cookies for a Thanksgiving dinner for the homeless; they studied the complex causes of poverty, challenged stereotypes of "poor people," and learned what local activists were doing to fight poverty. With their families, students came to school on a "snow day" the day before Thanksgiving to deliver food and work alongside adults to set up for a community meal. Cowhey, families, and children in The Peace Class have participated in a Children's March for Peace, organized a voter registration drive, and formed a small, parent-led group to investigate the Children Against [Land]Mines Program. Cowhey reflects honestly and in detail about the challenges, organization, and great rewards of working for a more just society.

As Margaret Mead said, "Never doubt that a small group of thoughtful, committed citizens can change the world. Indeed, it's the only thing that ever has."

CHAPTER 11

Advocating and Teaching Together

The Borderlands are physically present wherever two or more cultures edge each other, where people of different races occupy the same territory, where under, lower, middle and upper classes touch, where the space between two individuals shrinks with intimacy.

(Anzaldua, 1987, p. 21)

Sometimes schools and communities exist within the same cultural space; increasingly, though, there are borderlands of race, class, language, and other cultural aspects. Children are bused into schools far away from their neighborhoods; teachers commute to schools far away from theirs. In this chapter we'll learn how families and educators are traveling these physical, socioeconomic, racial, gendered, linguistic, spiritual, and educational borderlands

PARENT PARTNERSHIPS

Lessons on "Motherwit"

Mothers and grandmothers concerned about their young adolescents who attended an inner-city middle school in Baltimore formed With and For Parents. Donelda Cook and Michelle Fine (1995) learned some lessons on "motherwit" from talking with 12 African American mothers in the group. Cook and Fine detailed not only the pressures of living in unsafe areas and the effects of poverty on the families but also the strength and daily motherwit it took to raise their children safely and soundly. Too often they had to negotiate with nonsupportive educational institutions. For example, when their children got sent home from school in the middle of the day for some kind of infraction—one boy got ink on his pants—the schools didn't seem to consider that they would be walking through dangerous neighborhoods and that they'd come home to an empty house. Mothers often felt belittled by school personnel:

> I feel if I had not finished school, because I didn't, you shouldn't sneer at me . . . because I might have something that's knowledgeable to help you and we are supposed to be a helper for one another. . . . If I don't know, then you come to me and show me and help me . . . not to turn your nose up behind my back. . . . And I believe if [teachers] come as beings as one, no one higher than the other, you can find more parents coming in, coming in helping. (p. 128)

Cook and Fine (1995) concluded that the parents they interviewed, when they had the opportunity to talk and act together, were able to make connections "within and across communities and generations, 'with and for' other parents who couldn't, or wouldn't, be as active as they." The women "raised funds, pressured the principal, organized field trips, and established a Parent Resource Room in the middle school. At the foundation of their work lies a deep understanding of the complex lives of their neighbors, a thorough-going commitment to community life in African American communities" (p. 131). They noted that the kinds of things that schools sometimes offer, such as parenting classes, are not likely to be effective unless they are offered "within a broad based social movement committed to transforming the material and social circumstances of these women and their children" (p. 138).

Middle-class and wealthy parents like me have many avenues, formal and informal, for supporting and advocating for our children. As teachers, administrators, politicians, and school board members, we are often policymakers, or have access to them. Not all parents have such privilege. The mothers in With and For Parents banded together against instead of with the school. Why didn't "the school"—teachers, counselors, administrators—come to them, as the mother above suggested, "no one higher than the other"? Let's look at one teacher who did issue such an invitation to parents to create a borderland space across social class and immigration status.

"Learning the Rules of the Game"

Carmen Urdanivia-English, the teacher we met in Chapter 7, immigrated as an adult to the United States from Colombia. She invited parents of the Hispanic (as these parents self-identified) students she taught to discuss the issues of greatest interest to them concerning their children's education and well-being. Of the 37 children Urdanivia-English served, 23 parents met with her one Saturday each month to discuss how they could help their children be successful in school, with a focus on "learning the rules of the game" in their school.

Parents worked primarily in construction, in the poultry industry, and as homemakers. Their education in their home countries ranged from completing elementary school to postsecondary vocational/technical school degrees. Parents' goals and expectations were for their children to be successful in school and society, which included being a good person, helping others, and being good citizens, and to have a "better life," which parents defined as less strenuous jobs than their own with better salaries. The participants also voiced a variety of personal goals and expectations for their own future, including learning English, helping their children to study and become professionals in any area they chose, and supporting their families (Urdanivia-English, 2003).

Parents found schooling in the United States to involve different expectations of their children, as well as of them in terms of parental involvement. In their meetings, they articulated and explored these differences. The parents raised issues such as "domestic violence, child abuse, sexual education, helping their child with mathematics homework, and school/home relationships" (Urdanivia-English, 2003, p. 83). They also wrote in Spanish during meetings: thoughts about their children, reactions to things they had read or listened to—such as "Parable of the Eagle" (excerpted in James & Jongeward, 1996)—and evaluations of meetings and workshops. Some also wrote in journals at home.

Reflecting on the power of parents sharing important questions, experiences, and feelings with each other and with her, Urdanivia-English noted:

> From the beginning of our meetings, I encouraged the parents to write about any topic they wanted to explore in their lives that puzzled or worried them. In the large group, the parents appeared uncomfortable sharing their writings. I gave them a passage from my own journal about my upbringing. Upon reading it, the parents worked in small groups to talk about the journal. The groups drew on their own experiences to express their views about raising children and reported their conclusions to the large group. Through the remainder of the year, a few parents chose to write their journals in preparation for the meetings while some others verbally shared their views about each topic with the large group. (p. 83)

Out of the large meetings, a small writing group developed. Six Mexican mothers and grandmothers of Urdanivia-English's ESOL students decided to write about their children to counter stereotypes they felt some people in the United States held about them and their children. She explained, "Our focus was to offer a glimpse into what it is like to live in the United States as a Mexican immigrant (a Colombian immigrant in my case) and what it takes to rear (and teach) children in a culture so different and so often incomprehensible, a culture that evades us, that slips from our hands like wet soap" (Urdanivia-English, 2003, p. 121).

Urdanivia-English (2003) illustrated the power of these intimate conversations. Zunilda had just told her story of "crossing over" from Mexico to the United States. The circle of women was speechless, overwhelmed by the pathos of her story. Timidly, Sandra responded:

> I wrote a letter to my daughter. I tell her some things like what you just said. We came here *"a retar la vida,"* to dare and challenge life, risking our own lives, never mind that we did not speak the language or that we did not know the (local) customs. We go to work with courage and inner strength because we know that someone is waiting for us at home. . . . In the end, I am left with a question, *¿Es felíz aquí el niño?* [Is the child happy here?] Coming to the United States is like a two-edged sword. There are more opportunities to work here, and [when we are in our homeland] we believe that life here is wonderful; however, once we are here, we have to work long hours. Our children are left alone for the most part of the day, and we hardly see our spouses. And when we are working, we constantly wonder about our children. . . . People in our countries need to hear the true story of the immigrants, although I do not believe that will change their minds about coming here. (p. 140)

Parents discussed issues they themselves raised—a very different kind of parental involvement from that in "parenting" workshops designed by well-meaning educators who teach parents about how to read to their children, discipline them, help them with their homework, or better their own lives. Interestingly, parents chose many of these same topics. However, the parents not only chose these topics themselves; they contextualized them in their unique contexts, making the conversations highly meaningful.

Many participants in the group said they felt more confident and more capable of advocating for and teaching their children. Arturo was surprised when he heard another parent say she read to her child in Spanish. Teachers had warned him not to use Spanish in doing schoolwork with his child. Arturo shared his experiences with his son, initially believed to have a learning disability:

> At home I read to him in Spanish, to see if that will help him learn, and he becomes interested. "*¿Eso dice ahí, papá?* [Is that what that says, daddy?] *Sí, mijo. Eso dice aquí.* [Yes, my son. That is what it says.]. . . . So, that is what the letters say? What people talk, is that what they write on there?" he asked me, and I said, "Yes, that's it." (Urdanivia-English, 2003, pp. 196–197)

Action Opportunity: If possible, work in pairs of one teacher, one parent. Design an invitation to other parents to form a discussion group like the one Urdanivia-English and the parents of her students created. What forms would the invitation take—written, a phone call, in person? What examples might you include that would get other parents thinking about what they would want out of such a group? How could you keep the focus on student learning and at the same time be responsive to issues family participants raise?

PARENT-SCHOOL-COMMUNITY PARTNERSHIPS

Comprehensive Change in a Border Town

Our next borderland travel is to an actual border community. Patagonia is a beautiful little Arizona town (population 900) nestled between the Santa Rita and Patagonia Mountains 18 miles north of Nogales, Mexico. The elementary school is primarily Mexican and Mexican American, with 85% of the 83 students qualifying for a free or reduced-price lunch. The school staff and local site council developed a 5-year school improvement effort as a strong home–community–school partnership. Superintendent Susan Stropko (personal communication, December 31, 2003), who initiated the efforts, wrote, "Hundreds of family and community members join children to celebrate student success at Fall Harvest, Night Skies, and Celebrating Community—themes of school-wide instructional units through which students learn academic standards through integrated, hands-on curriculum. In a joyful atmosphere, families sit around a huge campfire on the playground, enjoying a meal and conversation with friends, and joining in the singing."

During the second phase, after families became more comfortable coming to the school for the community events, teachers invited them to evening workshops focused on their children's learning. The majority of students had at least one family member attending. As Stropko commented, "Teachers deliberately designed the next phase to avoid what they did not want: the school telling parents what they ought to do. Instead, teachers invited parents to engage in conversation about high quality education for their children." Facilitators met with small groups, where all parent voices could be heard to address these questions: What do you do as a parent that most helps your child to learn? What have you noticed that your child's teacher does that has helped your child to learn? What can we do together to help the children succeed? Parents made two requests, which were honored: establish multiage classes and keep sixth graders in the elementary building, where parents could continue their active involvement, rather than moving to the high school/middle school campus.

While it is impossible to create a causal link between any one aspect of school improvement and student achievement—the school also reformed literacy instruction and conduced teacher research—there are some impressive numbers to consider. Schools are judged based on the percentage of students who meet or exceed state standards on the AIMS (Arizona Instrument to Measure Standards) test, given in grades 3, 5, and 8 each year. Students in third grade went from 53% to 67% passing reading standards between 2000 and 2003; students in fifth grade went from 27% to 75% during the same period. The percentage passing the writing test went from 47% to 100% (third grade) and 9% to 75% (fifth grade), and in math the improvement was from 33% to 50% (third grade) and 27% to 63% (fifth grade). This was comprehensive school reform, and parents and community culture were an integral part.

The Comer Model for School Reform

Bringing families and communities together to transform schools led James Comer to create a different model of schooling, one in which the complexities not only of family lives but of school lives are tackled by teams of adults working together for children. As a social scientist, Comer recognized that schools cannot do all the work to reverse the shortcomings of society. I'll bet you knew that! In discussing the pervasive effects of race and class on children's education, Comer (1997) identified two American cultural myths that infect public education and influence public policy: that a person's success in life is determined by genetic intelligence and individual effort, and that Whites are more successful than Blacks. It is easy to see how many people connect these two myths with a "therefore." The first myth denies the power of supportive networks, preferential social structures, and biased public policy. The second myth marginalizes African American accomplishments and encourages racist and false assumptions about Black families. Comer called for a new strategy in which schools are more fully incorporated into the life, issues, and heart of the larger community, and in turn contribute in meaningful ways to that community.

Comer and his colleagues at the Child Study Center at Yale (Comer, 2001; Comer, Haynes, & Joyner, 1996) developed a highly successful model that involves families and community members in supporting child development and learning. Adults form school planning and management teams, parent teams, and student and staff support teams. Parents are actively involved in decisions that affect their children's physical, cognitive, psychological, language, social, and ethical well-being. They work with the principal, teachers, school psychologist, guidance counselor, school nurse, and community social service agencies. They focus on school plans that support the child as a whole person. Comer started with one school in a poor neighborhood in New Haven, Connecticut, and built a national model for school reform with an impressive record of achievement.

The Mother/Daughter Program

Another innovative and successful family–school–community initiative is the mother/daughter program, designed specifically for Latina mothers and daughters. Developed initially at the University of Texas at El Paso (UTEP) in 1986 in collaboration with the YWCA, this model focuses on the belief that "getting Latina girls to graduate from high school and to enter college requires a systematic partnership between the school, the family, and the university" (Delgado-Gaitan, 2004, p. 82). The UTEP model focuses on sixth-grade girls and their mothers. Together they "learn about their many life options by seeing success firsthand in successful Hispanic university students and career woman from every walk of life who participate in the program as role models" (http://academics.utep.edu/Default.aspx?tabid=20060). Shared activities include monthly meetings focusing

> **Action Opportunity:** One interesting way to look at James Comer's work is to read his memoir about his mother, *Maggie's American Dream: The Life and Times of a Black Family* (Comer, 1989). As you think and write about the influence of your own family on your education, you may see some parallels as well as some different social conditions. The first half of the book is Maggie's story, which Comer taped as she told it to him—a story of a Mississippi sharecropper's life marked by poverty and racism, but ultimately a story of resilience and determination to provide an education for her children. In the second half, Comer tells his educational story, including medical school and his work as a psychologist who has devoted his life to creating strong schools that are an integral part of the community, the kinds of African American communities in which he grew up.

on academic, personal, and community life as well as career development; university events, including Career Day, which features Latina professionals; community service projects, culminating in a leadership conference; a summer camp, where girls attend classes and sleep in dorms; and community activities including visits to art museums, libraries, medical centers, governmental offices, and other cultural and professional sites and events. Families remain active through the daughters' first year of college.

This is the kind of program that can be adapted in a variety of ways in different settings. It could be either/both parents and either sons or daughters; it could function without a university partner, although campus visits are critical; it could focus on any group with low high school graduation/college enrollment rates. The program has been adopted and adapted in Arizona, New Mexico, and California. One adaptation created by Carmen Contreras is "mother stories." Mothers meet monthly at a community center to discuss, write, and share powerful stories of their lives, stories about "faith, determination, and intelligence . . . to interpret the complex society in which they live and raise their families" (Delgado-Gaitan, 2004, p. 90).

So does this kind of effort pay off? Researchers followed the first group of sixth-grade girls in the UTEP program. When they were high school juniors, Delgado-Gaitan (2004) reported that 98% were still in high school (the dropout rate for Latinas is as high as 71% in some districts), 62% were in college-prep classes, 27% were in honors classes, and 76% were earning As and Bs. Another highly significant outcome of this program is that many of the mothers reported personal and professional growth, becoming leaders in the program, advocating effectively for their children's education, returning to high school, and enrolling in college (Delgado-Gaitan, 2004). One mother, Alma Garcia, shared her experience (translated from Spanish):

> Although I felt that I was supportive before, for Marina, it was fine with her to do the very least to get by. But this group taught me how to get my daughter motivated and to go the extra mile. . . . By the time that my daughter was in her first year of high school, she was so turned on about school that she began pushing me to get my diploma and enroll in college. . . . I am now enrolled at the state college and working toward my psychology major. . . . We both laugh at the thought of graduating from college together. It may just happen. (Delgado-Gaitan, 2004, p. 95)

Gentlemen on the Move

In a related program in Georgia, Deryl Bailey, a counseling professor at the University of Georgia, and his wife, Brad Bailey, a science teacher at Cedar Shoals High School, developed a program for African American males and their families. Gentlemen on the Move (GOTM) provides intensive support for African American males in fifth through twelfth grade. Through a Summer Academy, Saturday Academy, "Exam Lock-ins" to study for semester tests, and after-school tutoring, teachers and counselors in the program provide academic and social/personal counseling. Parents not only commit to making sure their sons study and attend all these events; they also commit their own time as Parents of Empowered Youth (PEY). In addition to attending all GOTM activities, they participate in monthly meetings and workshops that focus on the welfare of GOTM youth in school, in the community, and at home. They work closely with the GOTM staff in making decisions, establishing policies, and supporting each other. Finally, they schedule additional conferences with teachers throughout the year and, together with Bailey, monitor their sons' progress and performance. Participants now "on the move" through high school, college, and into careers often serve as mentors to younger GOTM participants.

So what differences do these intensive teacher–parent GOTM collaborations make? First, students know that there are adults—in their families, in their schools, and at the university—who care deeply enough about their success to give time after school, on weekends, and even through the night during the Exam Lock-ins. These adults are showing young GOTM participants not only that they believe in them but that they know how they are doing in school day by day, week by week. Second, Bailey and colleagues (Bailey, Phelps, Packer, & Hardin, 2006) have found that of 26 students who were in GOTM in the fall of 2004, 71% of them scored higher on exams than the class exam average. The class averages across 62 different exams were 74; the Gentlemen averaged 81%.

FOCUSED PARTNERSHIPS—MATH AND SPECIAL LEARNING NEEDS

What happens when this kind of powerful collaboration becomes even more focused on specific content—and what if it is—gasp—math? "Imagine parents getting together with other parents to do math and having fun doing it! Imagine parents helping their kids with math homework! Imagine families becoming microcommunities of math learners!" (http://mapps .math.arizona.edu/).

MAPPS, a Math Partnership

The above quote from the website is how the Math and Parent Partnership in the Southwest (MAPPS) program advertises, and parents *do* imagine. MAPPS provides workshops for parents and students to learn math together, minicourses for parents on mathematical concepts, and leadership development workshops where parents become facilitators for other parents. Among the many benefits are opportunities to connect learning at school and at home. As one parent said, "I think it is a really neat experience for [our children] because their school experience is not just an isolated part of their day. They can come home and say, 'OK, Mom or Dad is interested in this and cares and is involved.' It's really a good bridge between those two worlds."

The learning goes both ways. Teachers view parents as "intellectual resources" beyond "homework helpers" (Bernier, Allexsaht-Snider, & Civil, 2003). Teachers not only help parents understand math and develop ways of helping their children; they also learn what parents think about mathematics and how they use it in their everyday living, applying family funds of knowledge (http://mapps.math.arizona.edu/researchbasis.php). From being with parents in MAPPS workshops, teachers learned new strategies for teaching. They also developed different kinds of relationships. Middle school teacher Arlene Sumner explained, "I've never had the chance to work with parents like this before. It's always been kind of the parent on the other end of the phone line and the parent at the other end of the table, you know just somebody on the other side, not necessarily somebody who you really felt like you worked with" (Bernier et al., 2003, p. 17).

Universal Design for Learning

The relationship between children and families receiving special services is another important area needing the collaborative thinking and problem solving of parents and teachers. In your school, is there ever tension among parents of students with special needs, other parents, and teachers in regular-education or special-education classrooms? There is for many of the teachers and parents I've talked with, and I've certainly experienced some of that tension myself, both as a parent and as a teacher.

As parents, we want our children to be recognized as capable learners and also to be supported in areas where they have difficulty. We don't want them coloring or doing worksheets while other students are reading about dinosaurs or writing up a science experiment on the secret lives of worms. Neither do we want our children removed from the regular classroom or put in the "LD corner" with a special-education teacher or aide. We want our children to be full members of the community, with the support they need.

As teachers, we are committed to meeting the needs of every child, but this responsibility sometimes becomes overwhelming. Do we write six different lesson plans? When do we have time to collaborate with each student's other teachers? We don't want students to feel isolated or pushed out of our community of learners, but sometimes we don't know how else to accommodate for all needs.

One way educators are addressing these complex issues is in the area of Universal Design for Learning (UDL). Educators at the Center for Applied Special Technology (CAST) consortium work with regular classroom teachers and special educators to create "universally designed classrooms" (O'Neill, 2000). In such classrooms, students with special needs are not singled out with separate accommodations. Rather, teachers design learning experiences in such ways that many learners benefit from the strategies and materials.

O'Neill gave the example of reading technology that supported Matt, a first grader who struggled with decoding many words. With electronic versions of children's books, the computer program highlighted the words as Matt read aloud, pronounced difficult words when Matt clicked on them, and recorded the reading so he could hear himself reading the story. It also allowed a classmate who had motor impairment that kept her from holding a book to read the book independently and another child, an advanced reader with a short attention span, to read a higher-level book by setting the program to a faster pace. As O'Neill (2000) noted, "Very soon all the children in the classroom were grouping around Matt and the computer. These kids wanted to learn to read and write the way Matthew was learning to read and write" (p. 53).

As a parent, I would have loved to see this kind of UDL in my children's classrooms—all of my children, whether they excelled or struggled in reading, writing, or math. Elementary School Special-Education Coordinator Donna Palley, a Fellow in the CAST consortium, stressed that parents have a critical role in urging schools to create universally designed classrooms.

"Parents have a huge impact on school change, and a huge responsibility and an opportunity to take this information to their school district and to ask for it to help their child" (O'Neill, 2000, p. 56). For more information on Universal Design for Learning, contact the not-for-profit Center for Applied Special Technology at cast@cast.org or visit their website at http://www.cast.org.

Is Universal Design for Learning a principle that your school should adopt? What would it mean for learners—all learners? What role would parents take in designing and support UDL curricula and learning? This would be a great advocacy role for a group of parents and teachers—that's you!

Action Opportunity: Working in grade-level groups that include parents and both regular- and special-education teachers, list the range of needs in your current classroom(s). Consider cognitive, emotional, cultural, linguistic, and individual learning styles. Consult experts within your school and outside it to learn effective strategies for diverse learning needs. Develop a resource bank of strategies for engaging diverse learners, and, for each, look at how "universal" it might be at home or in a community setting as well as at school. Who might benefit in addition to students with identified special needs when you do the following:

- Record books and poems for a listening center (*To get you started, here are some possibilities: students with visual impairments, students who struggle with reading, students working on oral expression for a play or presentation, anyone who loves to be read to, and . . . who else?*)
- Use technology, such as graphics, photos, and music, for composing
- Encourage partners for some assignments
- Learn about local populations—for example, Cuban American, Native American, Hmong—and include their literatures
- Include texts written in two languages
- Encourage students to write in their home language or dialect as they learn a second language or dialect
- Plan active learning that involves drama, music, art, movement, or problem solving

CHAPTER 12

Transforming Schools Through "True Partnerships"

Para lo posible/*For what is possible*
Puedo hacer lo imposible./*I can do what is impossible.*
Para lo probable/*For what is probable*
Haré la realidad./*I will create reality.*
Y para los incrédulos/*And for the unbelieving*
Plantaré la semilla de lo posible./*I will plant the seed of what is possible.*
(Ted Slone, in Ada & Campoy, 2004, p. 187)

As we've explored throughout this book, there are many ways diverse families, students, educators, and community members can work together to create welcoming schools that support student learning. In this chapter, we'll look at actions you might take to create a "true partnership," as defined by home–school partnership expert Susan Swap (1993). A true partnership "is a transforming vision of school culture based on collegiality, experimentation for school improvement, mutual support and joint problem solving. It is based on the assumption that parents and educators . . . have a common goal: improving the school or supporting the success of all children in the school" (1993, p. 56).

"Transforming vision." If you aren't ready to take this giant step, you can stop reading now—go ahead, order the pizza, you've worked hard, and what Swap suggests is really going to push your school community.

TRANSFORMING SCHOOLS FOR STUDENT ACHIEVEMENT

Still here? I thought you might be. Here is Swap's (1993) framework for a "true partnership between home and school," along with my thoughts.

1. *Creating two-way communication.* We've looked at many ways of doing this throughout the book, including dialogue journals, discussion groups, better conferences, and learning about family funds of knowledge.
2. *Enhancing learning at home and at school.* Swap emphasized that "parents and educators develop an array of ways in which parents can be involved in and out of the classroom to enrich children's learning. Parents understand what is occurring in the curriculum and ways in which they can monitor, assist, or extend children's homework" (p. 58). One more time—it's not about PTA sign-in sheets.
3. *Providing mutual support.* What do parents need? What do teachers need? How will meeting these needs translate into student well-being and learning?
4. *Making joint decisions.* Swap emphasized that "parents and educators are involved in joint problem solving at every level: individual child, classroom, school, and district" (p. 58). And we're not talking about the school picnic here, but shared decision making about instructional philosophy, curricular programs, assessment, culturally relevant teaching—the issues that most affect student learning.

As we've seen in many examples throughout this book, there can be true partnerships among one teacher, the students, and their families. Swap

(1993) talked about those as limited partnerships for children's learning—but it may be all you, as one parent, one teacher, or a small group, can do at this time. A second option is a comprehensive approach comprised of networks of mutual support. For example, Martin Luther King Middle School in Boston offers a staffed parent center, parent information packets, parent volunteers in classrooms, a home read-aloud program, a School–Parent Council, and joint programs with community health centers. Kentucky has led the nation in establishing family resource centers, and other schools, districts, and states have implemented comprehensive family support networks.

If you have enough people interested in one or more schools and local community agencies, this might be a good place to start. I've been involved in such an effort for 5 years, the Partnership for Community Learning Centers. In the two partnership elementary schools there are now Family Engagement Centers, enrichment programs for all students, and university faculty working in the schools in ways ranging from complete literacy curriculum reform to special lessons on the lives of earthworms. We have accomplished a great deal as a partnership, including involving parents in hiring teachers and principals, raising test scores, and meeting Adequate Yearly Progress for 3 years after being on the brink of being labeled "failing schools." Parents have been involved in hiring principals and have served on school improvement teams, but we haven't gone to the third level, where many parents (not just a few) are actively involved in dialogue and decisions that change schools in fundamental ways.

The third level or path, according to Swap, is "restructuring schools for partnership and student achievement." These are two key concepts: (1) *restructuring schools*—"activities that change fundamental assumptions, practices, and relationships, both within the organization and the outside world, in ways that lead to improved student learning outcomes" (Conley, 1991, p. 49)—and (2) focusing on *student achievement*. How might schools cast their "transformative vision" on current school structures? Together, families and educators might question such fundamental assumptions and practices as fixed grade levels with new teachers each year, ability grouping and other kinds of tracking, retention, special-education pull-out models, time-bound classes, even whether the school building is the best place for learning. We're talking about the really big "but we've always done it this way" stuff.

Is that what your school and community need to do to make a real difference in the lives of the children you serve? As parents and teachers, are you willing to consider—to create—something radically different from your own schooling? If so, Swap offered (1993) some suggestions to get started.

1. Plan a sequence of family, school, and community collaborative events to develop a mission and goals, select a shared-decision-making council, create task forces to pursue priorities, assess progress, and plan next steps in a continuous cycle.
2. Select a framework for research and action. Our Partnership for Community Learning Centers started with a design team of school, university, and community members who visited schools throughout the country, read stacks of research, and made recommendations for comprehensive school reform from an extended-year calendar to site-based mathematics professional development.
3. Build readiness among faculty. We're talking about the folks who haven't taken this journey with you, who aren't at the same point you are, and may not even see the point—and this may be parents as well as faculty, central administrators as well as building principals.
4. Commit to a 3- to 5-year process. Our partnership began with a 5-year commitment from the superintendent, the dean of the College of Education, and the school board. Swap emphasized, as did we, that "There are no quick fixes when the task is changing long-standing patterns of relationships and behaviors."
5. Consider long-term consultations. Who are the resources you can draw on? What aspects might be led by parents? Community leaders? Educators in your district? Don't hire some big-name, big-money, one-shot guru; do tap into the expertise within your community, people who are willing to commit to the long process.

Action Opportunity: Where will you start? Divide into three groups with these tasks:

1. If we started with family, school, and community collaborative events to develop a mission and goals, here's how we might go about it.
2. If we started with building readiness among faculty, here's how we might go about it.
3. If we started with long-term consultation, here are some people we might contact.

Discuss and compare these starting points. Which one makes the most sense for you?

---

6. Secure and widen district support including policies, financial commitment, and public understanding and support. This is critical. In our partnership with two high-poverty schools, parents in a higher-socioeconomic school (yes, mostly university parents) became very vocal when the idea of a balanced school calendar threatened their children's long summer break. We no longer have a balanced calendar.
7. Recognize uniqueness. Make it your own. Adopting another model without adapting it will not work.

These goals and processes for restructuring schools for partnership and student achievement are a starting point, but as we've explored throughout this book, they are not enough to bring diverse families and schools together. We have to attend explicitly to the diversity within our unique communities.

TRANSFORMING SCHOOLS THROUGH CULTURALLY GROUNDED PARTNERSHIPS

Partnerships become culturally grounded when they are of the people, by the people, and for the people. It just won't work to guess at local cultures; essentialize and fix in place cultural knowledge; or reduce culture to food, festivals, and faces shaded gray on worksheets.

Sabrina Hope King, an assistant superintendent of a diverse school district and former teacher, and her colleague Lin Goodwin at Teachers College, Columbia University, have worked together to learn how to involve parents of diverse cultural backgrounds in their children's schooling. Their booklet, *Culturally Responsive Parental Involvement* (King & Goodwin, 2002), offers strategies for schools that have a sincere commitment to inviting every adult in a parenting role to be a meaningful part of their child's education. Some strategies include hiring or providing release time for a parent liaison (a teacher or parent); establishing a family room where families can meet, chat, drink coffee, read the paper—perhaps one written in their home language; and creating a resource notebook for both teachers and families with information such as available translators, community cultural organizations, places of worship, and other information.

Like Swap, King and Goodwin (2002) suggested that schools write a mission statement and goals that express its "commitment to meaningful and culturally responsive parental involvement" (p. 11). My favorite example of this occurred in a tiny rural school in Hart County, Georgia. Teachers didn't just write a mission statement and share it with families; they involved parents and children in the writing of the school's Covenant of Teaching and Learning. Through class meetings, students interviewing parents, and something akin to a town-hall meeting, all the stakeholders talked about what was important to them. They came up with the idea of making the covenant not only a living document but a walking one as well—they created a T-shirt featuring the school name as an acronym of their shared commitment:

> *Air Line Elementary School*
> *Covenant of Teaching and Learning*

> Students learn best when they have
> A   active learning opportunities
> I   interesting and meaningful curricula and individual instruction
> R   responsibility and choices
> L   learning environments that are positive
> I   instruction that challenges and supports all students
> N   networks with families and community
> E   enthusiastic, effective teachers

Learning from Family Surveys and Interviews

King and Goodwin also suggested that schools survey parents about their concerns, perspectives, and ideas with the intent not only of finding out what most parents think but also of really understanding the diversity of perspectives. This would be a great learning project for students, as the authors suggest. Students as young as first or second grade could design several questions to ask their parents or caregivers and could compile the information in various forms (charts, a class book, or a Web site). Teachers and students could discuss what kind of information they want to gather and why, what kinds of questions are appropriate and not rude or intrusive, and why parents might choose not to answer some questions (or any questions) due to concerns about their citizenship status or privacy.

As teachers and students think about questions, an important one to ask themselves is, *What kind of information can we gather that will help us become a stronger, culturally grounded learning community, one that includes us as students, our teachers and staff, and our families?* Our previous discussion of family engagement and funds of knowledge might give us some ideas.

> *Literacy and linguistic knowledge.* What languages or dialects are spoken at home? What kinds of oral language are practiced: storytelling, family sayings, parental "lessons" or *consejos* (lectures on

morality, values, or behavior), religious rituals, narrated audio- or videotapes to distant relatives? What kinds of written and visual language are common: favorite songs or poems, notes on the refrigerator, religious readings, newspapers, magazines, library books, DVDs, video games, television shows—especially those viewed together as a family?

Pedagogical knowledge. How do children in our family learn to do things? Think of things that your child has learned to do, such as playing a game, doing household chores, caring for animals, or learning the alphabet. How does your child learn best? What are some barriers that make learning hard? Who are the people that your child learns from best: brothers or sisters, parents, grandparents, other children, teachers, recreation leaders, others?

Skill knowledge. Revisit Chapter 3 to design questions about work—for example, agricultural, automotive, meat-processing, construction, child-care, medical, culinary—as well as spiritual, musical, artistic, scientific, cultural, domestic, and other funds of knowledge.

Community knowledge. What neighborhood or community groups, including informal ones, are important to your family? What does your child gain from these groups? What places does your child go in the community and what does he or she do there?

Knowledge beyond the local community. Does your family travel to visit relatives or for other reasons, and if so where? What connections do you have to family and friends outside your hometown? What do you think your child is learning or could learn from these visits or connections?

King and Goodwin (2002) suggested questions that could facilitate teacher–parent interaction as well as specific questions about the child's current schooling experience, such as these:

- Do you have scheduling issues, transportation needs, etc.?
- What are your working hours?
- What is working well for you and your child in this class or in this school?
- What should we do differently?
- What kinds of experiences or instructional materials would you like to be a part of your child's experience at school? (pp. 12–13)

Teachers and parents could follow up with more in-depth discussions on issues most relevant to their children's learning during conferences, when parents drop off or pick up their children, or via telephone or e-mail if parents have them. Teachers can also follow up by learning more about places and practices that parents mention in the surveys or, even better, invite teachers to accompany them to or paticipate in. These might include attending family, community, or religious events; shopping at local markets or in homes where family members sell food or crafts; or reading about traditions that are important to families such as daily prayers in the Muslim religion, child-naming practices in African American communities, or democratic governing structures in different Native American tribes. King and Goodwin proposed that schools could plan a series of parent–teacher seminars or parent–teacher team-building activities based on survey/interview findings.

Some educators have found questionnaires helpful in eliciting infor-mation and stories from parents and guardians. Edwards, Pleasants, and Franklin (1999) used a 50-item questionnaire about family life, learning, and parent–teacher relationships. The authors included a powerful pro-cess for writing and reflecting on the answers to these questions and con-structing instructional plans. I think Edwards and her colleagues would agree that it's important that such questionnaires be grounded in local cultures. Students, parents, and teachers can work together to create ques-tions and topics that invite conversation.

Here are my totally subjective guidelines for conversations with fami-lies, straight from my parent and grandparent heart. To my child's teacher:

1. I'd love to chat with you. I'd enjoy knowing you better and learn-ing more about you, and then I'd be willing to tell you more about myself.
2. Please don't ask me "judgment" questions—you know, like how much I read to my child, or if I take her to the library "regularly," or what time he goes to bed. I know what you want to hear. I'll ei-ther lie or avoid the question. If you'll excuse my bluntness, it re-ally isn't any of your business. Of course, some of that might come out in a conversation—you have trouble getting your kid away from the TV, too? Let's talk.
3. I love talking about my child, as long as I feel we are both consider-ing his best interests. I will shut down if you tell me she is lazy, dis-abled, too loud, too quiet—just about any label. I'll listen carefully if you tell me stories about my child in your classroom; maybe we can talk together about how we both interpret those stories.
4. I'll solve problems with you—these are my children, and nothing is more important to me, whether I show that to you or not. We can brainstorm options, discuss pros and cons, and come up with plans where we all have a part—you, me, and my child. If you come in with a "solution" and just want me to sign something, I probably won't.
5. We had a good talk and made a good plan. I really hope we can help each other follow through on it. How are we going to do that? Are

you going to call me, or e-mail, or could I drop by, say, on Fridays when I pick her up from school? Is this just one of those, "I tried to talk to the parent but she . . ." kind of visits? No, I didn't think so. You really care about my child. Say, my daughter is performing at a poetry slam next Friday night. You might be too busy, but I could save you a seat if you'd like to come. It's so important to her . . .

Learning Through Small-Group Discussions

In addition to surveying families and having one-on-one conversations, create opportunities for lots of small-group discussions. Matt Leighninger (2003), a senior associate of the Study Circles Resource Center in Ontario, advocates conversations with parents and community members in small groups rather than the traditional school-cafeteria-tired-parents-squirming-kids model still common for many parent meetings. In smaller groups, family members are more likely to share experiences and opinions, a lesson learned from those involved in race relations. Leighninger shared three important lessons gleaned from school administrators who pioneered small-group discussions with families.

1. *Encourage truly broad-based, large-scale participation.* Build a coalition of organizations (and their leaders) representing diverse community interests in education. If your school has a family resource coordinator, counselor, assistant principal, or parent liaison, this person can contact organizations such as neighborhood associations, businesses, religious organizations, and civic clubs. As an example, Leighninger (2003) noted, "In rural Harford County, Md., school leaders worked with community organizations to recruit 150 citizens. The project focused on the achievement gap between students of color and white students. The school district subsequently won a $1.1 million federal grant to implement the recommendations."
2. *Provide structure for the small-group discussions.* Leighninger recommended groups of 8 to 12 that meet several times, a facilitator who can help build trust, and ground rules set by the group to make sure every person is heard and no one voice dominates. Provide information on the issue and a clear goal for the meetings: What decisions will the group make? In Decatur, Georgia, more than 300 people participated in small-group discussions about redrawing elementary school boundaries. The groups used a guide detailing redistricting options written by a committee of parents and other citizens with the help of a local nonprofit, Common Focus. Leighninger concluded, "Because the project allowed people to examine

the options in an even-handed, analytical way, the school board was able to adopt a redistricting plan with less acrimony than school leaders had expected."

3. *Ask participants to take action, not just make recommendations.* Some policy decisions cannot be made by teachers and parents, but it is surprising how many can be influenced by this powerful coalition. In my hometown, the board of education cut back the assistant principal's position at a small elementary school. A group of teachers and parents with persuasive data argued effectively for a change in policy. Leighninger (2003) recommended that small groups who have met several times on a specific issue then merge in a large-group meeting to "move the ideas to an action stage." He cited examples of actions including "construction of new schools in Florida and Illinois, creation of a regional school district in New Hampshire, averting a teachers' strike in Arkansas, devising initiatives for bridging the achievement gap in Calvert and Montgomery counties, Maryland, passing school bond issues in Kuna, Idaho, and South Kitsap, Wash., and launching tutoring programs and other grassroots projects."

A SCHOOL THAT BECAME A FAMILY

A wonderful example of a school that restructured in dramatic ways is Gardendale Elementary School, a Latino school in a high-poverty neighborhood in San Antonio. Teachers and parents collaborated to create Gardendale Family, a school-within-a-school where children and their siblings stay together from kindergarten through sixth grade. Azucena Torres, a third-grade teacher, described this restructuring of school as building on "the strong traditions of the extended family within the Mexican American culture" to provide a "multigenerational web of adults (grandparents, parents, aunts, and uncles) and older children (brothers, sisters, cousins) who assume responsibility for each other and especially for younger children" (Torres & Pérez, 1998, p. 32).

The Gardendale Family included teachers and other school personnel, all of whom assumed responsibility for all the children in the Family. For example, Mr. Campos, the custodian, read with Victoria weekly throughout her years at Gardendale; she went from being a "potential problem in first to a contributing member of the Family in fourth grade" (p. 32) within this supportive family. Parents and other relatives were involved throughout the school, helping teachers and children in the halls and cafeteria, and attending Family Celebrations of student accomplishments that were so popular that the extended families of teachers as well as of students attended.

Families described many benefits to being members of the Gardendale Family. Those with more than one child developed especially close relationships because their children had the same teachers. Often two or three teachers conferred with a family together, discussing all the children in the family; thus "teachers impact the learning and interactions of the whole family" (p. 33). Parents and other family members became familiar with teachers' expectations; older siblings were more able to help younger ones because they had the same teacher.

Parents could visit all their children who attended the school by going to one hallway where Family classrooms were always open to them. Mrs. Cuenca explained, "I like to go when there is nothing special, and you can just see what the children are doing on a regular day" (p. 35). Some parents participated directly in the classrooms, where they read to children, listened to children read, and planned thematic studies that involved parents in the content as well as educational field trips.

A school that became a family. Gardendale Family teachers and parents looked at the "givens" of schooling (isolated grade levels, families at home and teachers at school) and said, "This is not working for our children." They envisioned school as an extended family and transformed their vision into a reality.

Action Opportunity: What is your shared vision for your children, your students? How will you "plant the seed for what is possible" to transform your school?

CREATING WELCOMING SCHOOLS—HOW WILL YOU?

This book has been an attempt, as I said in the Introduction, to spin strands of communication from which to weave the web of caring that supports each child, each teacher, and each family so that all children learn to their full potentials. Together we have seen the power of the research that tells us, "When programs and initiatives focus on *building respectful and trusting relationships* among school staff, families, and community members, they are more effective in creating and sustaining connections that *support student achievement"* (Henderson & Mapp, 2002, p. 43, emphasis added).

So now it is up to you. You have read and talked. You have shared memories of school, cultural memoirs, and family funds of knowledge. Perhaps you have argued, laughed, even cried. You have tried some actions, succeeded, failed, and learned from each attempt more about each other as a unique and diverse school family. On notable occasions you have achieved dialogue—really heard and respected a differing viewpoint, seen another cultural perspective. Your partnership has begun.

Only begun. One teacher and the families in his room are dialoging in journals. The sixth graders are interviewing veterans of the civil rights movement for an oral history project. Several mothers and grandmas are eager to start a mother/daughter program. The principal has ordered several of the books recommended in this book for another study group next year.

But what are all of you—families, educators, community members, and students—going to do that makes your learning community the inclusive and welcoming family you want it to be? What is your vision for 5 years, 10 years, from now, and what will you do tomorrow to begin living that vision? What will you design that is unique to your community? How will you stay on track? How will you know if you are making a difference in your child's, your student's, learning?

These are questions I cannot answer, but you can. And when you do, when you start making changes that start making a difference for kids, would you let me know? Email me (jobethal@uga.edu). I really want to know.

Additional Resources for Families and Educators

Parents and teachers together have tremendous power. That power is strengthened greatly with pertinent information—for example, successful partnerships in similar schools, research on closing the achievement gap, details of programs that might be adapted in your district. We have learned from the work of many educators throughout this book—Karen Hankins, Sarah Lawrence-Lightfoot, Betty Shockley and Barbara Michalove, Concha Delgado-Gaitan, and Norma Gonzáles, Luis Moll, and Cathy Amanti. This appendix provides several additional resources for your next steps.

Hopkins, R. (1997) *Educating black males: Critical lessons in schooling, community, and power*. Albany: State University of New York Press.

Hopkins reviewed and provided addresses and contact information for over 35 alternative schools and community programs for African American males, such as Paul Robeson African-Centered Academy in Detroit and Dr. Martin Luther King Jr. African American Immersion Academy in Milwaukee. Many programs involved mandatory home visits and/or parent volunteer time in the schools. Mr. Stevens, a parent Hopkins interviewed from Nijia Afrocentrist School, explained, "At Nijia, we are a whole unit, the principal, students, teachers and staff, parents, and the entire local community. Everyone cares about everyone" (p. 85).

National Black Child Development Institute (NBCDI) (http://www.nbcdi.org/programs/programs.asp).

This excellent resource for parents and teachers provides information about educational programs including the following:

- *Love to Read* focuses on early literacy.
- *African American Parents' Project* helps children cope with crises.
- *Center on the Social and Emotional Foundations for Early Learning* strengthens child care and Head Start.

- *Entering the College Zone* helps students and their parents navigate college application processes.
- *Cross Cultural Partners* promotes partnerships among African American and Latino communities; this collaboration of NBCDI and the National Council of LaRaza is creating powerful alliances benefiting families and children in Miami, Los Angeles, and New Jersey.
- *Parent Empowerment Project* (PEP) supports parents as their children's first teachers; the curriculum is determined by parents. PEP invites active participation through role playing, art, and music; it also incorporates African American culture, history, values, and achievement. NBCDI leaders conducted discussions with African American parents and grandparents to design PEP. They noted that too often programs for low-income African American families "attempted to transplant aspirations and ideals into their lives as if to fill a void" (Moore & Barbarin, 2003, p. 58)

Parents for Public Schools (PPS) (www.parents4publicschools.com).

Started by 20 parents in Jackson, Mississippi, in 1989, PPS is a national organization of community-based chapters with a diverse membership. PPS values the following:

- Public education as an important part of American life, as an essential element of a democracy, and for the richness in diversity it offers our children
- Effective parent involvement as critical to strong public schools
- Constructive involvement of parents in the governance of schools and as a bridge between the schools and the community
- Parents as committed *owners* of, rather than passive consumers in, public schools
- Improvement of public education for every child, not just our own

The founding chapter in Jackson, working collaboratively with school district personnel, tackled the problem of students dropping out of high school, many in ninth grade. PPS analyzed the reasons, enlisted parents and educators from district high schools, and even got the mayor involved. They created ninth grade as a "school within a school" to ease the transition to high school, assigned counselors to every ninth grader, and provided professional development for teachers. The dropout rate decreased 28% in 4 years. The PPS leadership institute educates parents on how to identify and address student learning needs, such as enrolling students in Advanced Placement courses, improving achievement on graduation exams, and helping students develop individualized graduation plans.

These parents and educators, working together through a parent-initiated, parent-run group, are indeed "proactive problem solvers" (Womack, 2005).

Weiss, H. B., Faughnan, K., Caspe, M., Wolos, C., Lopez, M. E., & Kreider, H. (2005). *Taking a closer look: A guide to online resources on family involvement*. Harvard Family Research Project (www.finenetwork.org).

This excellent resource of applied research from the Harvard Family Research Project's Family Involvement Network of Educators (FINE) can be downloaded free. The guide includes information on knowledge and professional development, standards for family involvement from various professional organizations, and how to contact programs and organizations. It also includes reports and links to family-focused programs, such as Even Start, Families and Schools Together, and the National Parent School Partnership Program of the Mexican American Defense and Educational Fund; school-focused programs, such as the Comer Process, PTA, and the School, Family, Community Partnership; and community-focused projects, such as ACORN (Association of Community Organizations for Reform Now), the Coalition for Community Schools, and Communities in Schools.

Weiss, H. B., Kreider, H., Lopez, M. E., & Chatman, C. M. (Eds). (2005). *Preparing educators to involve families: From theory to practice*. Thousand Oaks, CA: Sage.

Case studies are often a great way to discuss difficult issues that may feel "too close to home." Heather Weiss, Holly Kreider, Elena Lopez, and Celina Chatman are researchers with the MacArthur Network on Successful Pathways Through Middle Childhood. They developed this book of short cases from the School Transition Study of 400 diverse, low-income K–5 children from three sites across the United States. The short teaching cases of problems and issues that arise among children, parents, and teachers are excellent for discussion among faculties and families for two reasons. First, the issues, while locally situated, are ones that are common in many schools (e.g., "A Special Education Plan for Anabela: Does Supporting Her Needs Mean Holding Her Back?" and "My Favorite Subject Is Lunch: Motivating a Disengaged Student"). Second, each case contains the perspectives of all the key players—parents, teachers, and students. The authors' definition of family involvement is consistent with the one I've promoted in this book: "the activities that families engage in to support their children's learning, whether at home, at school, or in the community" (p. xii).

References

Ada, A., & Campoy, I. (2004). *Authors in the classroom: A transformative education process.* New York: Allyn & Bacon.

Allen, J., Fabregas, V., Hankins, K., Hull, G., Labbo, L., Lawson, H., Michalove, B., Piazza, S., Piha, C., Sprague, L., Townsend, S., & Urdanivia-English, C. (2002). PhOLKS lore: Learning from photographs, families, and children. *Language Arts, 79*(4), 312–322.

Allen, J., & Labbo, L. (2001). Giving it a second thought: Making culturally engaged teaching culturally engaging. *Language Arts, 79*(1), 40–52.

Allen, J., Michalove, B., & Shockley, B. (1993). *Engaging children: Community and chaos in the lives of young literacy learners.* Portsmouth, NH: Heinemann.

Allen, L., & Thompson, K. (2005, February). Democratic service-learning. *Talk It Up: Advocating for Service Learning*, Edition 10. [Newsletter]

Allison, D. (1992). *Bastard out of Carolina.* New York: Dutton.

Amanti, C. (2005). Beyond a beads and feathers approach. In N. Gonzáles, L. Moll, & C. Amanti (Eds.), *Funds of knowledge: Theorizing practices in households, communities, and classrooms* (pp. 131–142). Mahwah, NJ: Erlbaum.

Angelou, M. (1994). *My painted house, my friendly chicken, and me.* New York: Clarkson Potter.

Anzaldua, G. (1987). *Borderlands la frontera: The new mestiza.* San Francisco: Aunt Lute Books.

Bailey, D., Phelps, R., Packer, C., & Hardin, J. (2006). Empowering youth. In *Education* (pp. 9–11). Athens: University of Georgia College of Education.

Banks, J. (1993). Multicultural education: Historical development, dimensions and practice. *Review of Research in Education, 19,* 3–50.

Barnhardt, R. (1990). Two cultures, one school: St. Mary's, Alaska. *Canadian Journal of Native Education, 17*(2), 54–65.

Bartoli, J. (2001). *Celebrating city teachers: How to make a difference in urban schools.* Portsmouth, NH: Heinemann.

Bernier, E., Allexsaht-Snider, M., & Civil, M. (2003, April). *Teachers, parents and mathematics: Exploring contexts for collaboration and partnership.* Paper presented at the annual meeting of the American Educational Research Association, Chicago.

Billig, S. H. (2000). Research on K–12 school-based service-learning: The evidence builds. *Phi Delta Kappan, 81,* 658–664.

Boethel, M. (2003). *Diversity: School, family, and community connections.* Annual report of the National Center for Family and Community Connections with Schools. Austin: Southwest Educational Development Laboratory.

Boethel, M., Averett, A., & Jordan, C. (2000). *Thriving together: Connecting rural school improvement and community development*. Austin: Southwest Educational Development Laboratory.

Bragg, R. (1997). *All over but the shoutin'*. New York: Pantheon.

Bronfenbrenner, U. (1994). *Making human beings human: Bioecological perspectives on human development*. Thousand Oaks, CA: Sage.

Brown, R. (2005). "Grandma, you got time? Papa, you got time? I want to read to you." In C. Dozier, P. Johnston, & R. Rogers (Eds.), *Critical literacy/critical teaching: Tools for preparing responsive teachers*. New York: Teachers College Press.

Buley-Meissner, M. (2002). The spirit of a people: Hmong American life stories. *Language Arts, 79*(4), 323–331.

Campano, G. (2007). *Immigrant students and literacy: Reading, writing, and remembering*. New York: Teachers College Press.

Casper, V., & Schultz, S. (1999). *Gay parents/straight schools: Building communication and trust*. New York: Teachers College Press.

Christensen, L. (2000). *Reading, writing, and rising up: Teaching about social justice and the power of the written word*. Milwaukee: Rethinking Schools.

Cisneros, S. (1989). *The house on Mango Street*. New York: Vintage.

Comer, J. (1989). *Maggie's American Dream: The life and times of a Black family*. Plume.

Comer, J. P. (1997). *Waiting for a miracle: Why schools can't solve our problems—and how we can*. New York: Dutton.

Comer, J. P. (2001). Schools that develop children. *The American Prospect, 12*(7). (http://www.prospect.org/print/V12/7/comer-j.html).

Comer, J. P., Haynes, N. M., & Joyner, E. T. (1996). The school development program. In J. P. Comer, N. M. Haynes, E. T. Joyner, & M. Ben-Avie (Eds.), *Rallying the whole village: The Comer process for reforming education* (pp. 1–26). New York: Teachers College Press.

Compton-Lilly, C. (2003). *Reading families: The literate lives of urban children*. New York: Teachers College Press.

Conley, D. (1991). What is restructuring? Educators adapt to a changing world. *Equity and choice, 7*(2 & 3), 46–55.

Cook, D., & Fine, M. (1995). "Motherwit": Childrearing lessons from African American mothers of low income. In B. Swadener & S. Lubeck (Eds.), *Children and families "at promise": Deconstructing the discourse of risk*. Albany: State University of New York Press.

Cowhey, M. (2006). *Black ants and Buddhists: Thinking critically and teaching differently in the primary grades*. Portland, ME: Stenhouse.

Delgado-Gaitan, C. (2001). *Power of community: Mobilizing for family and schooling*. New York: Rowman & Littlefield.

Delgado-Gaitan, C. (2004). *Involving Latino families in schools: Raising student achievement through home–school partnerships*. Thousand Oaks, CA: Corwin.

Dixon, D. (1993). *Writing your heritage: A sequence of thinking, reading, and writing assignments*. Berkeley: National Writing Project.

Dozier, C., Johnston, P., & Rogers, R. (2006). *Critical literacy/critical teaching: Tools for preparing responsive teachers*. New York: Teachers College Press.

DuBois, W. E. B. (1949/1970). The freedom to learn. In P. S. Foner (Ed.), *W. E. B.*

Du Bois Speaks (pp. 230–231). New York: Pathfinder. (Original work published 1949)

Edelsky, C. (1999). Education for democracy. In J. Allen (Ed.), *Class actions: Teaching for social justice in elementary and middle school* (pp. 147–156). New York: Teachers College Press.

Edwards, P., Pleasants, H., & Franklin, S. (1999). *A path to follow: Learning to listen to parents.* Portsmouth, NH: Heinemann.

Fanelli, S. (2001). *My map book.* New York: Harper.

Fields-Smith, C. (2005). African American parents before and after *Brown*. *Journal of Curriculum and Supervision, 20*(2), 129–135.

Frank, C. (2003). Mapping our stories: Teachers' reflections on themselves as writers. *Language Arts, 80*(3), 185–195.

Freire, P. (1970). *Pedagogy of the oppressed.* New York: Continuum.

Freire, P. (1994). *Pedagogy of hope.* New York: Continuum.

Gay, G. (2000). *Culturally responsive teaching.* New York: Teachers College Press.

Gibbons, G. (1997). *Click!* New York: Little, Brown.

Gonzáles, N., Moll, L., & Amanti, C. (Eds.). (2005). *Funds of knowledge: Theorizing practices in households, communities, and classrooms.* Mahwah, NJ: Erlbaum.

Hankins, K. (1998). Cacophony to symphony: Memoirs in teacher research. *Harvard Educational Review, 68*(1), 80–95.

Hankins, K. (2003). *Teaching through the storm.* New York: Teachers College Press.

Henderson, A., & Mapp. K. (2002). *A new wave of evidence: The impact of school, family, and community connections on student achievement.* Austin: Southwest Educational Development Laboratory.

Hensley, M. (2005) Empowering parents of multicultural backgrounds. In N. Gonzáles, L. Moll, & C. Amanti (Eds.), *Funds of knowledge: Theorizing practices in households, communities, and classrooms* (pp. 143–152). Mahwah, NJ: Erlbaum.

Hicks, B., Montequin, L., & Hicks, J. (2000). Learning about our community: From the Underground Railroad to school lunch. *Primary Voices, 8*(3), pp. 26–33.

Holbrook, T. (2003). *Home work.* Unpublished manuscript.

Igoa, C. (1995). *The inner world of the immigrant child.* New York: St. Martin's Press.

James, M., & Jongeward, D. (1996). *Born to win: Transactional analysis with gestalt experiments.* Reading, MA: Perseus. (Original work published 1971)

King, S. H., & Goodwin, A. L. (2002) *Culturally responsive parental involvement: Concrete understandings and basic strategies.* New York: American Association of Colleges for Teacher Education.

Kunjufu, J. (2005). *Keeping Black boys out of special education.* Chicago: African American Images

Ladson-Billings, G. (1994). *The dreamkeepers: Successful teachers of African American children.* San Francisco: Jossey-Bass.

Lamott, A. (1999). *Traveling mercies: Some thoughts on faith.* New York: Anchor.

Lareau, A. (2003). *Unequal childhoods: Class, race, and family life.* Berkeley: University of California Press

Lawrence-Lightfoot, S. (2003). *The essential conversation: What parents and teachers can learn from each other.* New York: Random House.

Leifield, L., & Murray, T. (1995). Advocating for Aric: Strategies for full inclusion. In B. Swadener & S. Lubeck (Eds.), *Children and families "at promise": Deconstructing the discourse of risk* (pp. 238–261). Albany: State University of New York Press.

Leighninger, M. (2003). Working with the public on big decisions. *The School Administrator*. Retrieved December 30, 2006 (http://www.aasa.org/publications/sa/2003_11/focus_Leighninger.htm).

Lyon, G. E. (1999). *Where I'm from, where poems come from*. Spring, TX: Absey & Co.

Mattingly, D. J., Radmila, P., McKenzie, T. L., Rodriguez, J. L., & Kayzar, B. (2002). Evaluating evaluations: The case of parent involvement programs. *Review of Education Research, 72*(4), 549–576.

McAuliff, D. (1994). *Deaths of Sybil Bolton (an American history)*. New York: Crown.

McBride, J. (1996). *The color of water: A Black man's tribute to his White mother*. New York: Riverhead.

McIntyre, E. & Kyle, D., Moore, G., Sweazy, R. A., & Greer, S. (2001). Linking home and school through family visits. *Language Arts, 78*(3), 264–272.

McKee, K. (1988). *Framing our past and crafting our present*. In G. Wolfe (Ed.), *The program for the colored museum* (pp. 18–20). Atlanta: Tom Kepler.

Meacham, S. (2003, January 5). *From Frederick Douglass to Tupac: "Fugitive literacy" and its insights for inquiry and academic identity*. Paper presented at the Qualitative Inquiry Group Conference on Interdisciplinary Qualitative Studies, Athens, GA.

Mercado, C. (2005). Reflections on the study of households in New York City and Long Island: A different route, a common destination. In N. Gonzáles, L. Moll, & C. Amanti (Eds.), *Funds of knowledge: Theorizing practices in households, communities, and classrooms* (pp. 233–257). Mahwah, NJ: Erlbaum.

Min, A. (1994). *Red azalea*. New York: Berkeley.

Moll, L., Amanti, D., Neff, D., & Gonzáles, N. (1992). Funds of knowledge for teaching. *Theory Into Practice, 31*(2), 132–141. Reprinted in Gonzáles, N., Moll, L., & Amanti, C. (Eds.). (2005). *Funds of knowledge: Theorizing practices in households, communities, and classrooms* (pp. 71–88). Mahwah, NJ: Erlbaum.

Moore, E., & Barbarin, O. (2003). Respecting the voices of parents: How the spirit of excellence Parent Empowerment Project connects with African American parents. In J. Mendoza, L. Katz, A. Robertson, & D. Rothenberg (Eds.), *Connecting with parents in the early years* (pp. 57–66). Urbana-Champaign, IL: Clearinghouse on Early Education and Parenting.

Morgan, K. (1981). *Children of strangers: The stories of a Black family*. Philadelphia: Temple University Press.

Morrell, E. (2004). *Becoming critical researchers: Literacy and empowerment for urban youth*. New York: Peter Lang.

Morris, A. (1995) *I am six*. Needham Heights, MA: Silver, Burdett, & Ginn.

Moutoussamy-Ashe, J. (1993). *Daddy and me: A photo story of Arthur Ashe and his daughter, Camera*. New York: Knopf.

Murphy, P. (1994). Antonio: My student, my teacher. *Language Arts, 1*(2), 75–88.

Null, E. H. (n.d.) "Llano Grande Center's oral history project sparks cultural and economic renewal in Texas's Rio Grande Valley." Retrieved August 10, 2005, from the Rural School and Community Trust website (http://www.ruraledu .org/projects/project0400.html).

Nye, C., Turner, H., & Schwartz, J. (n.d.) *Approaches to parent involvement for improving the academic performance of elementary school age children.* Retrieved August 1, 2006, from Campbell Corporation's website (http://www.campbellcollaboration.org/ doc-pdf/Nye_PI_Review.pdf).

O'Neill, L. (2000). Moving toward the vision of the universally designed classroom. *The Exceptional Parent, 9*(30), 52–56.

Orellana, M., Reynolds, M., Dorner, L., & Meza, M. (2003). In other words: Translating or "para-phrasing" as a family literacy practice in immigrant households. *Reading Research Quarterly, 38*(1), 12–34.

Paratore, J. (2001). *Opening doors, opening opportunities: Family literacy in an urban community.* Boston: Allyn & Bacon.

Patterson, L., Baldwin, S., Gonzales, R., Guadarrama, I., & Keith, L. (1999). To claim our ignorance and make new friends: Collaborative family inquiry and culturally responsive literacy teaching. *Networks: An On-line Journal for Teacher Research.* Retrieved August 12, 2006, from http://www.oise.utoronto.ca/ ~ctd/networks/journal/Vol%202(2).1999oct/article1.html.

Perez, D. (2005). Voces del corazón: Voices from the heart. *The Quarterly of the National Writing Project, 27*(2), 24–28.

Rayburn, S. (2003). *Social worlds of learning differently: A parallel study of two families.* Unpublished doctoral dissertation, University of Georgia, Athens.

Rodriguez, R. (1982). *Hunger of memory: The education of Richard Rodriguez.* New York: Bantam.

Rogers, J. (2000). *Invitations to literacy: A case study of a child with autism.* Unpublished doctoral dissertation, University of Georgia, Athens.

Rothstein, R. (2004). *Class and schools: Using social, economic, and educational reform to close the Black-White achievement gap.* Washington, DC: Economic Policy Institute.

Shockley, B. (1993). Extending the literate community: Reading and writing with families. *The New Advocate, 6*(1), 11–23.

Shockley, B., Michalove, B., & Allen, J. (1995). *Engaging families: Connecting home and school literacy communities.* Portsmouth, NH: Heinemann.

Sis, P. (2000). *Madlenka.* New York: Farrar.

Skrtic, T. (1991). The special education paradox: Equity as the way to excellence. *Harvard Educational Review, 61*(2), 148–206.

Sleeter, C. (1996). *Multicultural education as social activism.* Albany: State University of New York Press.

Smith, M. C., & Elish-Piper, L. (2002). Primary-grade educators and adult literacy: Some strategies for assisting low-literate parents. *Language Arts, 56*(2), 156–165.

Swap, S. (1993). *Developing home–school partnerships: From concepts to practice.* New York: Teachers College Press.

Thompson, G. (2004). *Through ebony eyes: What teachers need to know but are afraid to ask about African American students.* San Francisco: Jossey-Bass.

Torres, A., & Pérez, B. (1998). Community building. *Primary Voices, 6*(1), 32–39.

Torres, M. (1998). Celebrations and letters home: Research as an ongoing conversation among students, parents and teacher. In A. Egan-Robertson & D. Bloome (Eds.), *Students as researchers of culture and language in their own communities* (pp. 59–68). Cresskill, NJ: Hampton.

Urdanivia-English, C. (2003). *The praxis of learning: Negociando the rules of parental involvement with Hispanic parents.* Unpublished doctoral dissertation, University of Georgia, Athens.

U.S. Bureau of the Census. (2000). *The foreign born population in the United States, 2000* (CHP-L98). Washington, DC: Author.

Valdés, G. (1996). *Con respeto: Bridging the distances between culturally diverse families and schools: An ethnographic portrait.* New York: Teachers College Press.

Vasquez, V. (2004). *Negotiating critical literacies with young children.* Mahwah, NJ: Erlbaum.

Weiss, H. B., Faughnan, K., Caspe, M., Wolos, C., Lopez, M. E., & Kreider, H. (2005). *Taking a closer look: A guide to online resources on family involvement.* Harvard Family Research Project. Retrieved August 8, 2005, from www.finenetwork.org.

Weiss, H. B., Kreider, H., Lopez, M. E., & Chatman, C. M. (Eds). (2005). *Preparing educators to involve families: From theory to practice.* Thousand Oaks, CA: Sage.

Weissbourd, R. (1996). *The vulnerable child: What really hurts America's children and what we can do about it.* New York: Perseus.

Williams, K. (1991). *Galimoto.* New York: HarperTrophy.

Winston, L. (1997). *Keepsakes: Using family stories in elementary classrooms.* Portsmouth, NH: Heinemann.

Womack, S. (2005). Parents as proactive problem solvers. *National Dropout Prevention Center/Network Newsletter, 17*(2), p. 5.

Woodson, C. G. (1933/2005). *The mis-education of the Negro.* Mineola, NY: Dover.

Index

About the Author

JoBeth Allen conducts collaborative action research with teachers who are exploring issues of educational equity and social justice in relation to literacy teaching and learning. She is a professor at the University of Georgia in Language and Literacy Education, where she teaches poetry, composition, difficulties in literacy teaching and learning, critical pedagogies, and a week-long qualitative research writing retreat in the mountains of north Georgia. She co-directs the Red Clay Writing Project. Her books include three collaborations with teacher–researchers Betty Shockley and Barbara Michalove: *Engaging Children, Engaging Families,* and *Engaging Teachers.* Other collaborations with teacher–researchers include *Exploring Blue Highways: Literacy Reform, School Change, and the Creation of Learning Communities* and *Class Action: Teaching for Social Justice in Elementary and Middle School.* Most importantly, she is Grace's and Luke's grandma.